RIVERSIDE COMMUNITY COLLEGE
1916

DATE DUE

MY 24 '96			
DE 20 '96			
MR 26 '97			
AP 1 '9			

DEMCO 38-296

P9-CJK-309

U.S. CRIMINAL JUSTICE INTEREST GROUPS

Greenwood Reference Volumes on
American Public Policy Formation

These reference books deal with the development of U.S. policy in various
"single-issue" areas. Most policy areas are to be represented by three types of
sourcebooks: (1) Institutional Profiles of Leading Organizations, (2) Collection of
Documents and Policy Proposals, and (3) Bibliography.

Public Interest Law Groups: Institutional Profiles
Karen O'Connor and Lee Epstein

U.S. National Security Policy and Strategy: Documents and Policy Proposals
Sam C. Sarkesian with Robert A. Vitas

U.S. National Security Policy Groups: Institutional Profiles
Cynthia Watson

U.S. Agricultural Groups: Institutional Profiles
William P. Browne and Allan J. Cigler, editors

Military and Strategic Policy: An Annotated Bibliography
Benjamin R. Beede, compiler

U.S. Energy and Environmental Interest Groups: Institutional Profiles
Lettie McSpadden Wenner

Contemporary U.S. Foreign Policy: Documents and Commentary
Elmer Plischke

U.S. Aging Policy Interest Groups: Institutional Profiles
David D. Van Tassel and Jimmy Meyer, editors

U.S. CRIMINAL JUSTICE INTEREST GROUPS

/ / /

Institutional Profiles

Michael A. Hallett
and
Dennis J. Palumbo

GREENWOOD PRESS
WESTPORT, CONNECTICUT • LONDON

Riverside Community College
Library
AUG '94   4800 Magnolia Avenue
Riverside, California 92506

Library of Congress Cataloging-in-Publication Data

Hallett, Michael A.
    U.S. criminal justice interest groups : institutional profiles /
Michael A. Hallett and Dennis J. Palumbo.
        p.   cm.
    Includes bibliographical references (p.   ) and index.
    ISBN 0–313–28452–0 (alk. paper)
    1. Criminal justice, Administration of—United States—Societies,
etc. 2. Criminal justice, Administration of—United States—Citizen
participation. 3. Pressure groups—United States. I. Palumbo,
Dennis James, 1929–   . II. Title. III. Title: US criminal justice
interest groups. IV. Title: United States criminal justice interest
groups.
HV9950.H35   1993
364′.06′073—dc20   92–45070

British Library Cataloguing in Publication Data is available.

Copyright © 1993 by Michael A. Hallett and Dennis J. Palumbo

All rights reserved. No portion of this book may be
reproduced, by any process or technique, without the
express written consent of the publisher.

Library of Congress Catalog Card Number: 92–45070
ISBN: 0–313–28452–0

First published in 1993

Greenwood Press, 88 Post Road West, Westport, CT 06881
An imprint of Greenwood Publishing Group, Inc.

Printed in the United States of America

The paper used in this book complies with the
Permanent Paper Standard issued by the National
Information Standards Organization (Z39.48–1984).

10 9 8 7 6 5 4 3 2 1

For
Dad and TL,
who helped me through.

And for Hal,
a true friend and teacher.

—MAH

For Sachiko, who
has seen the best of times and
the worst of times. Hopefully, there
have been more of the former.

—DJP

CONTENTS

/

PREFACE

/

Given the size of the criminal justice system in the United States it might be expected that there would be a large number of interest groups attempting to fashion criminal justice policy. Although we both have been doing criminal justice research and teaching for a number of years we were surprised to find that there has been very little research about criminal justice interest groups. Thus, this reference volume breaks new ground. In it, we have tried to include all of the major groups that might be called "interest groups" in each of the three major areas of criminal justice: law enforcement, courts, and corrections.

First, however, we wrestled with how to define "interest groups." In the area of criminal justice the major players do not all fall into what might be defined as an interest group in the classical sense. The common definition of an interest group is a group of people who have common interests and who pressure government to adopt policies that favor their interests. We found that this conception must be broadened in order to be able to include groups that do not simply lobby government officials but who also raise consciousness about criminal justice issues that had been ignored in the past. One example is the National Organization for Women, which succeeded in raising the public's consciousness about domestic violence and thereby getting policy changes aimed at treating this as a crime rather than just a "family matter." Another is Mothers Against Drunk Driving, who succeeded in getting penalties for driving while intoxicated increased. These are not interest groups in the same sense as the American Farm Bureau in the area of agricultural policy.

Another important dimension of interest groups are those that are a part of the criminal justice system rather than outside of it. An example here is the Fraternal Order of Police whose members are among the most influential in shaping policy, particularly in regard to law enforcement.

After settling on a definition that includes more than lobbying and that is not limited to groups outside of the criminal justice system, we started a search of major sources for the names of groups that might fit this broader conceptualization. We first consulted the *Encyclopedia of Associations* (1992) for groups under the headings of criminal justice, law enforcement, corrections, and courts. Then we checked hearings on criminal justice issues held by the U.S. Congress over the past several years. We checked articles and books that conceivably dealt with criminal justice interest groups (and didn't find many). Finally, we searched the computerized data files of LEXIS/NEXIS which contain national newspaper stories over the past ten years. The last was the most helpful source.

After compiling an initial list of interest groups, we developed a questionnaire and mailed it to each one on the list. The questionnaire returns helped us to describe many important aspects of the groups, including the number of members, their budgets, their policy issue interests, the levels of government they interact with most, what methods they use to try to influence criminal justice policy, and how successful they believe they are in their efforts. We also were able to obtain a lot of information about the groups from the LEXIS/NEXIS files.

The three major areas within the criminal justice system are well represented in the resulting list in the book: law enforcement, courts, and corrections. In addition, we found that a considerable number of religious organizations, as well as governmental agencies themselves, have an interest in criminal justice policy.

Last, we wish to emphasize that this volume is offered only as a "resource book." It is not intended to be an exhaustive catalogue of interest groups operating in the criminal justice field. How could it be? In fact, upon being asked to undertake this project for Greenwood Press we were initially loathe to do so: "There's no way we can get them all," we said. "There are too many important groups—and we'll go crazy trying to rank them in order of importance, etc. Forget it."

After doing some initial research, however, we discovered that no such reference existed for criminal justice. We could contribute to the work of practitioners, students, academics, and even the lives of prisoners with such a book. In short, the lack of research in the area came to inspire us—and, for this reason, we decided to take our *own* approach, including many prisoner's groups, women's groups, student groups, religious groups, as well as most of the larger, prominent groups. Thus, this book should be viewed only as a resourceful starting point—not as a comprehensive examination of all criminal justice interest groups. We have tried to be diverse in our inclusion of groups and strongly feel that more work is needed in this area.

An asterisk (*) indicates that a group or organization mentioned in passing has a complete profile in this volume.

We owe a debt of gratitude to all the organizations that took the time to fill out and return their questionnaires to us. The book could not have been completed without them. We also would like to thank our editor, Mildred Vasan, who made a number of helpful suggestions that have greatly improved the book. We come away from our work with the conclusion that the area of criminal justice interest groups is essentially unexplored territory, and we hope to be able to pursue it further in the future.

INTRODUCTION

―――――――――――― / ――――――――――――

Criminal justice in the 1980s and early 1990s was a growth industry. The number of offenders in federal and state prisons more than doubled from 1982 to 1992. By mid-1992 there were 1.25 million offenders behind bars and an additional 3.2 million on probation or parole. During 1990, nearly 17,000 publicly funded state and local law enforcement agencies were operating in the United States. Local police departments had operating expenditures of $20.6 billion and employed 460,000 persons on a full-time basis during 1990. State police departments had an additional 77,000 persons working full time with $3.7 billion in operating expenditures.

The average cost to keep one person incarcerated for a year in 1992 was about $25,000, and the average cost to keep one person on probation for a year was $5,000. When we multiply these by the number of people under each form of corrections, the total costs are about $47 billion per year. Added to the law enforcement costs mentioned above brings the total to about $71 billion a year. And this does not include the costs of courts and prosecution, nor the costs of building prisons and jails.

The amounts spent on criminal justice are staggering. What role do interest groups play in determining how these vast sums are spent? The answer to this question depends partly on how "interest groups" are defined. When defined the traditional way as "those organizations that are entirely or partially dedicated to influencing the formulation and execution of public policy in the areas of crime and criminal justice administration" (Fairchild, 1981, 183) then the main answers are "we don't know" and "not much." Oddly enough, for a public policy area that has for years been close to the top of concern for the public and that absorbs a large portion of public expenditures, there has been very little research on interest groups in criminal justice. Fairchild (1981, 182) writes:

"What has been missing in the study of the politics of criminal justice . . . has been systematic empirical research about general questions related to interest-groups influence and operations." Moreover, the research that has been done is contradictory. Jacob (1984, 5–6) claims that

the crime problem never attracted much attention from interest groups except when legislation to ban handguns was proposed; then the National Rifle Association charged in full force. Otherwise, law enforcement legislation and administration were espoused mostly by police groups and their allies, who had little clout in the political arena. The fight against crime was mounted by pygmies rather than giants in the world of interest groups.

Jacob is referring to crime in American cities. When the scene is shifted to the federal level, the conclusion is quite different. Here a large number of big and powerful interest groups get involved during such things as the revision of the federal criminal code. These include the American Bar Association (ABA), American Civil Liberties Union, U.S. Chamber of Commerce, AFL-CIO, and during the 1980s conservative groups such as the Moral Majority (now defunct). These are hardly pygmies.

Thus, one of the difficulties when we try to answer the question about the impact that interest groups have on criminal justice policy is that the criminal justice system is so fragmented. In addition to the many layers of government (federal, state, county, city, and town) at which policy is made, there are the multiplicity of types of law enforcement, court, and corrections agencies. In such circumstances, it is difficult to generalize.

More important, however, is the traditional definition of criminal justice interest groups. The definition quoted above is narrow and restrictive. It includes only those groups that are "dedicated to influencing the formulation and execution of public policy in the areas of crime and criminal justice administration." Many, if not most, groups that influence criminal justice policy are only partially dedicated to influencing criminal justice issues, and thus will have influence on only a single issue of concern to them. No wonder, then, that some research concludes that "notably absent from this list (of groups that were influential in federal criminal code reform) were groups whose specific interest was criminal justice" (Stolz, 1984, 97). Instead, legal associations, federal government agencies, general social reform groups, civil rights organizations, and business and labor organizations were influential (i.e., the ABA, Justice Department, Chamber of Commerce, and the AFL-CIO). Moreover, only nine of the over one hundred interest groups that testified during the hearings were considered to be influential (i.e., succeeded in achieving their goals).

Our survey of criminal justice agencies, which had forty-nine valid responses, tended to support this. Only nine, or 18 percent, said that they were very effective in getting changes in the legislation they wanted. These are the ABA, American Correctional Association, Correctional Education Association, Federal Criminal

Investigators Association, National Committee to Abolish Repressive Legislation, National Criminal Justice Association, National Organization to Reform
Marijuana Laws, National Rifle Association, and Justice Fellowship. However,
twenty-three, or 47 percent, said that they were moderately effective, eleven
said they had relatively little effect, and six said they had no effect at all.
Moreover, most (40) said that they were very (21) or moderately (19) active in
trying to influence public policy. Thus, while they tried to influence policy, they
did not perceive that they were very effective. Very few used lobbying (only 7)
or direct mailing (6). Most used education as their principal means of convincing
policy makers to support them.

Our survey found that the majority of criminal justice interest groups (69%)
say that they take a position on legislation. They all are nonprofit organizations
and most (79%) have under 5,000 members (the median size is 3,214 members).
Most (45%) have fewer than five staff members, although twelve (21%) had
more than twenty-five staff members. Forty-eight percent receive their financial
support from their members; the rest receive most of their support from multiple
sources and 16 percent say government is their principal source of support. The
median budget is $87,000, but the distribution is bimodal with 42 percent having
$10,000 or less annually and 24 percent having $5 million or more.

Criminal justice in the United States is predominantly state and local rather
than federal. Although the federal government finances a large amount of local
law enforcement, the overwhelming amount is raised and spent at the state and
local level. The types of interest groups that have the greatest amount of influence
at the federal level are different than those that have influence at the local level.
At the federal level, the American Bar Association, the American Civil Liberties
Union, the Justice Department, and business groups have the most influence
(Stolz, 1984). At the local level, it is groups composed of criminal justice
professionals (i.e., law enforcement personnel, corrections officials, prosecuting
attorneys) that play a similar role. These local groups are what Jacob calls the
pygmies of interest groups. But they are no doubt powerful in shaping criminal
justice policy at the local level.

Police, for example, through their groups such the Fraternal Order of Police,
are powerful in local communities. They use a variety of tactics to gain support
for law enforcement, but one main tactic is working closely with the media to
influence the public's perception of crime. And, since crime is what news people
call a "grabber," the media are eager to play up crime stories on television and
in newspapers. Most of the information the media gets about crime comes from
the police. And, in turn, the great majority of people (95%) learn about crime
from the mass media (Graber, 1980, 49–50). The media gives a great deal of
emphasis to crime. Crime and justice topics averaged 25 percent of all offerings
in the newspapers in Chicago during a one-year period studied by political
scientist Doris Graber (1980). Television devotes 20 percent of local station time
to crime, while 13 percent of national programming features crime. The media
also focuses on murder, robbery, and assault, which maximizes public fear of

crime (Esltp and Macdonald, 1984). This focus is often coupled with an image of the criminal as a young male, usually African American or another minority (Graber, 1980, 55). The police readily provide stories that support these images, and this in turn provides fuel for politicians who run on "get tough on crime" platforms. Thus, the police as an interest group have an impact on public policy but not in the classical interest group lobbying manner. Instead, they along with the media help change the public's image of crime and contribute to fear of crime. This, in turn, is used by politicians running for office. During the 1980s, the result was passage in many states of harsh criminal codes containing mandatory sentencing. Our conclusion is that criminal justice policy is formed more by these forces than by interest group pressure in the classic sense.

At the state level, criminal justice policy is "conceived by small numbers of influential legislators, administrators, and interest group representatives and state legislators" (Fairchild, 1981, 188). The interest groups that have the most influence are those that represent prosecuting attorneys and police. The important point to note here is that those who benefit most from an increased emphasis on criminal justice (police, prosecutors, and corrections officials), are also the ones who have the most influence in shaping policy at the state level, either through the submission of budget requests and by providing data and information to legislators and council members or through their professional associations.

Legislation isn't the only way that criminal justice policy is shaped. The courts play a large role as well. Disadvantaged groups, such as the poor and minorities, do not have as much influence on legislative policy as they do before the courts (Olson, 1990). The disadvantaged groups tend to use the courts because other arenas are not as receptive to them and tend to initiate a larger proportion of litigation than other groups. This is not to say that the more powerful groups do not use the courts; courts are also used by more powerful groups to enforce gains won politically.

Interest group activity is usually thought of as lobbying before legislatures or filing amicus curiae in court cases. Another, perhaps more important form of interest group activity is making the public and elected officials aware of an issue and defining it as a crime. For example, domestic abuse, sexual harassment, and child abuse were not considered crimes until various women's groups made the public and public officials aware of the problems. Domestic violence went virtually unnoticed until the National Organization for Women (NOW), as well as radical feminists, made people aware of it. Women from NOW task forces accompanied battered women to courts and assisted them in pressing criminal charges against their spouses (Pleck, 1987, 187). Emphasis on rape also emerged out of and contributed to the growth of radical feminism (Pleck, 1987, 185). Rape was defined by feminists as an act of domination, as a form of "mass terrorism" against randomly chosen women victims (Brownmiller, 1975; La Free, 1989, 46–47). In 1973, the New York Radical Feminists called for judicial review of courtroom procedure in rape cases, stronger punishment for rapists, and they also demanded a broadened definition of rape to include husbands and boyfriends. By 1976, new state laws concerning rape and wife abuse were passed in New York. These established more effective court procedures and increased penalties.

Thus, groups that would not normally be thought of as criminal justice interest groups (i.e., NOW) have had a significant impact on criminal justice policy. In contrast to other policy areas (i.e., agriculture) where there are interest groups devoted specifically to that policy area (i.e., American Farm Bureau Federation), most groups that have an impact on criminal justice policy are not exclusively devoted to criminal justice issues or devoted to only a single issue (i.e., National Rifle Association). Most important, probably the most influential criminal justice interest groups are not really interest groups in the traditional sense at all but, instead, professional associations of members of criminal justice agencies such as police, probation and parole officers, and prosecutors. These associations, although pygmies when measured against what is usually considered to be a traditional interest group, have enormous influence in shaping public policy. But they do it in more indirect ways, by working quietly with small numbers of influential legislators and administrators and working to enact legislation on a consensual basis. Not many legislators are willing to challenge police or prosecutor associations when an important part of the criminal code is being considered.

In conclusion, it can be said that interest group activity in criminal justice is unique. There are few if any groups that devote themselves exclusively to criminal justice issues; many groups that are influential at the national level will be concerned with criminal justice only episodically; and the most influential actors are the ones who have most to gain by changes in criminal justice policy but who are not really interest groups in the classic sense of that term.

The information about the policy positions of the interest groups was obtained from answers to a questionnaire mailed to organizations, from congressional hearings, and by a computer search of NEXIS (which is a computerized service of newspaper stories). Data about the interest groups was obtained through the questionnaire (see Appendix A) mailed to one hundred agencies. We received sixty-two responses for a response rate of 62 percent. In addition, a search for information about all agencies questioned was conducted over the NEXIS Electronic Information Service and pertinent information on current activities taken from there. Additional information was gleaned from a foray into the legislative record, the 1991 Omnibus Crime Bill, and the *Encyclopedia of Associations*.

Information about the governing structure of the agencies is difficult to obtain without a great deal of field research. In general, however, it can be said that for the smaller organizations—which comprise the majority of criminal justice interest groups—members of the executive boards are selected informally with relatively little participation by the general membership. The procedures for selecting board members for the larger agencies are more formal, including ballots mailed out to members containing information about the candidates—however, the percentage of members who vote in these elections seems to be small. Given this tendency, it is likely that those who are elected may not necessarily be representative of the larger membership in all ways.

U.S. CRIMINAL JUSTICE INTEREST GROUPS

A

———————————— / ————————————

ACADEMY OF CRIMINAL JUSTICE SCIENCES (ACJS)
Northern Kentucky University
402 Nunn Hall
Highland Heights, KY 41076
(606) 572–5634

ORGANIZATIONAL HISTORY/DEVELOPMENT

Founded in 1963 as a private, nonprofit organization devoted to the professional advancement of criminal justice practitioners, the Academy of Criminal Justice Sciences (ACJS) publishes academic journals and promotes research in the field of criminal justice/criminology. The organization is composed of various criminal justice professionals, including administrators, probation officers, corrections officers, students, and professors. Today the ACJS has some 2,500 members and an annual budget of $200,000. The ACJS was formerly known as the International Association of Police Professors (1971).

MISSION STATEMENT/PURPOSE

"To foster excellence in education and research in the field of criminal justice in institutions of higher education; to encourage understanding and cooperation among those engaged in teaching and research in criminal justice agencies and related fields; to provide a forum for the exchange of information among persons involved with education and research in the criminal justice field; to serve as a clearinghouse for the collection and dissemination of information related to or produced by criminal justice education and/or research programs; to foster the highest ethical and personal standards in criminal justice educational programs as well as in operational agencies and allied fields."

KEY POLICY ACTIVITY/CONCERNS

The ACJS sponsors and promotes research in the fields of criminal justice and criminology. The organization offers annual awards for outstanding research and holds an annual meeting/conference.

FURTHER INFORMATION/RESOURCES

The ACJS publishes two academic journals, the *Journal of Criminal Justice Education* (semiannually) and *Justice Quarterly* (quarterly). In addition, the organization publishes a quarterly newsletter titled *ACJS Today*.

AID TO INCARCERATED MOTHERS (AIM)
Jean Fox, Executive Director
95 Berkeley Street
Boston, MA 02116
(617) 695–1588

ORGANIZATIONAL HISTORY/DEVELOPMENT

Founded in 1980 as a private, nonprofit organization devoted to helping incarcerated mothers maintain their family ties, Aid to Incarcerated Mothers (AIM) works primarily in the Boston, Massachusetts, area. Currently, AIM has a full-time staff of five.

MISSION STATEMENT/PURPOSE

None provided.

KEY POLICY ACTIVITY/CONCERNS

AIM provides transportation to family members of incarcerated mothers for in-prison visits, counsels women on their rights in prison, seeks to assist incarcerated mothers in asserting these rights, and offers support to mothers once released from prison. The organization also acts as a resource agency for other groups interested in the plight of women prisoners and sponsors public awareness campaigns and speakers on the topic of female prisoners.

FURTHER INFORMATION/RESOURCES

AIM publishes a newsletter three times per year titled *Staying Together*.

ALLIANCE FOR JUSTICE
See Judicial Selection Project.

AMERICAN ASSOCIATION FOR CORRECTIONAL PSYCHOLOGY (AACP)
Robert R. Smith, President
West Virginia University
College of Graduate Studies
PO Box 1003
Institute, WV 25112
(304) 766–1929

ORGANIZATIONAL HISTORY/DEVELOPMENT

Since its founding in 1953 as an affiliate of the American Correctional Association,* the American Association for Correctional Psychology (AACP) has expanded to nine regional groups with over 400 members. Formerly the American Association of Correctional Psychologists (1983), the AACP is a private/non-profit organization composed of psychological practitioners in the field of corrections, academics, and researchers working in the American correctional system. The AACP currently has a staff of seven and an annual budget of about $10,000.

MISSION STATEMENT/PURPOSE

"The American Association for Correctional Psychology (AACP) was founded in 1978 to bring together into one body all behavioral body scientists who are interested in the psychology of crime and the criminal justice system."

POLICY ACTIVITY/CONCERNS

The AACP participates in no direct lobbying nor activism and has no separate board of directors (from the American Correctional Association*). The group has two working committees, one devoted to "ethics" and the other to "standards." The organization has taken no positions on specific legislation but is viewed as an authority with regard to the psychological welfare of inmates. For example, in 1987 the AACP actively commented on a rash of jail suicides across the country and stressed the damaging nature of many of our antiquated, overcrowded prisons ("The Self-Imposed Death Sentence: Jail Suicide," *Psychology Today*, June 1987).

FURTHER INFORMATION/RESOURCES

The AACP publishes a quarterly journal, *Criminal Justice and Behavior*, and a newsletter, *Correctional Psychologist*. See also the American Correctional Association.

AMERICAN ASSOCIATION OF CORRECTIONAL PSYCHOLOGISTS
See American Association for Correctional Psychology.

AMERICAN ASSOCIATION OF WARDENS AND SUPERINTENDENTS
See North American Association of Wardens and Superintendents.

AMERICAN BANKERS ASSOCIATION (ABA)
1120 Connecticut Avenue, NW
Washington, DC 20036
(800) 872-7747

ORGANIZATIONAL HISTORY/DEVELOPMENT

Founded in 1875, the American Bankers Association (ABA) began when a group of bankers met in Saratoga Springs, New York, for the purpose of discussing strategies related to enhancing the efficiency and capacity of the U.S. banking industry. Today the ABA's "Office of the General Counsel" oversees the ABA's litigatory and legislative initiatives. The General Counsel's Office monitors legislation at the national, state, and local levels relevant to the banking industry. This office also prepares research reports, submits amicus curiae briefs, and provides testimony in legislative hearings/sessions. The key operational body of the ABA, however, is its board of directors, and the supreme authority of the organization is its General Convention—each member institution having one vote. The combined assets of ABA's member banks comprise approximately 95 percent of the U.S. banking industry total, with over 1,000 individual member banking institutions. The ABA considers itself "the voice of the American banking industry."

MISSION STATEMENT/PURPOSE

"To enhance the role of America's commercial banks as the preeminent providers of banking services. This mission is accomplished through efforts such as federal legislative and regulatory activities, legal action, research, communications and education and training programs."

KEY POLICY ACTIVITY/CONCERNS

The ABA is a prominent voice in Senate committee hearings on such topics as international drug money laundering and regulation of the banking industry in the aftermath of the "savings and loan crisis."

During the Senate investigation of the Savings and Loan crisis, the ABA submitted a research report titled "Savings and Loan Association Regulatory Reform: Action Recommendations and Historical Perspective" to members of Congress. The ABA committee that drafted this report, the FSLIC Oversight Committee of the ABA, recommended restricting the scope and jurisdiction of the Federal Home Loan Bank Board, under whose supervision the Savings and Loan scandal took place. Regulation of the banking industry has been perhaps the key justice-related concern of the ABA in recent years.

FURTHER INFORMATION/RESOURCES

The ABA publishes a weekly newspaper, the *ABA Bankers Weekly*, and maintains a daily toll-free recorded message service ([800] 424–2871) offering recent information about federal legislative and regulatory action important to the banking industry.

References

Abt Associates. (1979). *The Federal Reserve Membership Problem: Impact on Banks: A Study for the American Bankers Association*. Washington, DC: American Bankers Association.

American Bankers Association. (1982). *American Bankers Association Literature Index*. Washington, DC: American Bankers Association.

Bartlett, Donald L., and James B. Steele. (1992). *America: What Went Wrong?* Kansas City, MO: Andrews and McMeel.

Golembe Associates. (1982). *Commercial Banking and the Glass-Steagall Act: Prepared for the American Bankers Association*. Washington, DC: American Bankers Association.

Hope, C. C. (1980). *The American Bankers Association: Providing Unity and Leadership to the Banking Industry*. New York: Newcomen Society in North America.

AMERICAN BAR ASSOCIATION SECTION OF CRIMINAL JUSTICE (ABA-SCJ)

1800 M Street, NW, 2nd Floor South Lobby
Washington, DC 20036
(202) 331–2260

ORGANIZATIONAL HISTORY/DEVELOPMENT

Since its founding in 1920, the American Bar Association (ABA) Section of Criminal Justice has broadened its mission to include prosecutors, defense lawyers, judges, academics, corrections personnel, and others working in the criminal justice system who are not lawyers. This commitment to a more "system-wide" approach has led the ABA to be more heavily involved in issues of practitioner concern and policy implementation rather than simply strict policy formation. The Section of Criminal Justice now has a staff of ten and a budget of over $750,000.

MISSION STATEMENT/PURPOSE

"Founded to provide a forum within the American Bar Association for discussion of criminal justice issues and for persons practicing criminal law to interact."

KEY POLICY ACTIVITY/CONCERNS

The ABA's Section of Criminal Justice monitors issues relevant to the administration of criminal justice, particularly those in the courts, and assists lawyers at the appellate level. The ABA Section of Criminal Justice has been particularly active on issues of the death penalty as applied to juveniles, the language of the 1988 Anti-Drug Abuse Act, and the development of procedural guidelines and standards for the administration of justice by the courts. The ABA Section of Criminal Justice has supported gun control, sentencing reform legislation, limits to federal habeas corpus provisions in death penalty cases, and the exclusionary rule. The section has been opposed in the past, however, to the establishment of minimum mandatory sentences, congressional efforts to "federalize" many state crimes, and efforts to radically alter habeas corpus strictures. The ABA's periodic publication of its Criminal Justice Standards drafting project has also made a major contribution to the field of criminal justice. All lobbying done by the Section of Criminal Justice is done on behalf of the ABA.

FURTHER INFORMATION/RESOURCES

The ABA Section of Criminal Justice publishes *CJS*, a quarterly magazine, numerous pamphlets and information packets, and conducts educational seminars for practicing attorneys on subjects ranging from the appeals process to federal RICO statutes.

References

American Bar Association. (1986). *American Bar Association Criminal and Juvenile Justice Policies: A Roadmap for State Legislators and Policy Makers*. Washington, DC: American Bar Association.
————. (1980). *American Bar Association Standards for Criminal Justice*. Boston: Little, Brown.
Smith, Barbara E. (1991). *Strategies for Courts to Cope with the Caseload Pressures of Drug Cases: Executive Summary*. Chicago: American Bar Association.
————. (1989). *Improving Enforcement of Court-ordered Restitution: Executive Summary*. Chicago: American Bar Association.

AMERICAN BAR FOUNDATION (ABF)
750 N. Lakeshore Drive
Chicago, IL 60611
(312) 988–6500

ORGANIZATIONAL HISTORY/DEVELOPMENT

Established in 1952 as a private, nonprofit organization devoted to research and education in the legal field, the American Bar Foundation (ABF) assists the legal profession by acting as a sociolegal research agency. The ABF currently has a full-time staff of about forty and an annual budget of roughly $3 million.

MISSION STATEMENT/PURPOSE

"To conduct basic empirical research on law and legal institutions."

KEY POLICY ACTIVITY/CONCERNS

The ABF conducts research on law and the legal profession and sponsors sociolegal research. Further, it publishes one of the leading scholarly journals in the area of sociolegal research.

FURTHER INFORMATION/RESOURCES

The ABF publishes the quarterly journal *Law and Social Inquiry*.

AMERICAN CORRECTIONAL ASSOCIATION (ACA)
8025 Laurel Lakes Court
Laurel, MD 20707–5075
(301) 206–5100
(800) ACA–JOIN

[For Accreditation Information]
4321 Hartwick Road
College Park, MD 20740
(301) 699–7600

ORGANIZATIONAL HISTORY/DEVELOPMENT

Founded in 1870, the American Correctional Association (ACA) is the oldest and largest private correctional organization in the United States. The association has become the preeminent membership organization for corrections professionals and is very active at all levels of policy formation. Today the ACA has over 25,000 members and a staff of ninety. ACA is made up of wardens, superintendents, parole board members, and administrators as well as correctional officers and other correctional staff. The ACA was formerly known as the National Prison Association and the American Prison Association, respectively. Former U.S. President Rutherford B. Hayes was elected the National Prison Association's first president.

MISSION STATEMENT/PURPOSE

"The ACA seeks to improve correctional standards including selection of correctional personnel, care, supervision, education, training, employment, treatment, maintenance of correctional facilities and post-release adjustment of inmates. Sponsors training seminars, workshops, and correspondence courses for correctional personnel and administrators."

KEY POLICY ACTIVITY/CONCERNS

American Correctional Association frequently testifies before congressional committees on issues related to corrections such as the "Congressional Alternatives Act of 1989," the "Omnibus Crime Bill of 1991," and on issues related to prison overcrowding. The ACA maintains a "Division of Standards and Accreditation" which is responsible for the organization's policy statements, guidelines, and programs. The organization sponsors numerous training programs, seminars, correspondence classes, accreditation certificates, and management training for correctional personnel. The ACA currently maintains dual membership roles with most state correctional associations and conducts research and compiles statistics on the state of corrections in the United States.

FURTHER INFORMATION/RESOURCES

American Correctional Association publishes *Corrections Today*, a bimonthly journal; *Directory of Institutions*; *National Jail and Adult Detention Directory*; and *On the Line*, the ACA newsletter.

References

American Correctional Association. (1980). *Issues in Juvenile Delinquency*. College Park, MD: American Correctional Association.

Congress of Correction. (1980). *Proceedings on the One Hundred and Tenth Annual Congress of Correction of the American Correctional Association*. College Park, MD: American Correctional Association.

AMERICAN CRIMINAL JUSTICE ASSOCIATION (ACJA)

P.O. Box 61047
Sacramento, CA 95806
(916) 484–6553

ORGANIZATIONAL HISTORY/DEVELOPMENT

Formerly called Lambda Alpha Epsilon (1970), the American Criminal Justice Association (ACJA) is an organization devoted to the professional advancement of criminal justice practitioners through training seminars, workshops, and physical fitness activities. ACJA's membership includes college students studying in the criminal justice field, working law enforcement officers, and attorneys. ACJA currently has over 4,000 members and an annual budget of about $60,000. About 75 percent of ACJA's members are college students.

MISSION STATEMENT/PURPOSE

"Dedicated to furthering the professional standards of criminal justice, fostering assistance and understanding of the problems and objectives of agencies devoted to the administration of criminal justice."

KEY POLICY ACTIVITY/CONCERNS

The ACJA sponsors scholastic research paper competitions, workshops and seminars, presents annual awards, and publishes the *Journal of the American Criminal Justice Association*. The organization is most widely known for its yearly, week-long conferences in which students of criminal justice and law enforcement officers meet to test physical strength, agility, shooting skills, and knowledge of the criminal justice system.

FURTHER INFORMATION/RESOURCES

American Criminal Justice Association publishes *Journal of the American Criminal Justice Association* semiannually.

AMERICAN FRIENDS SERVICE COMMITTEE (AFSC)
1501 Cherry Street
Philadelphia, PA 19102
(215) 241–7000
(215) 241–7060

ORGANIZATIONAL HISTORY/DEVELOPMENT

Founded in 1917 by the Religious Society of Friends (Quakers), the American Friends Service Committee (AFSC) is one of the most active of all criminal justice "interest groups." This ecumenical organization is essentially a "peace church" active in the area of criminal justice and is a confederation of individuals dedicated to peaceful resolution of conflict. Now separated from the Quakers (Quaker Committee on Jails and Justice*) and staffed by individuals sharing belief in nonviolence as a means to resolve conflict, the AFSC has nine regional groups across the country and a staff of 330.

MISSION STATEMENT/PURPOSE

None provided.

KEY POLICY ACTIVITY/CONCERNS

The AFSC has been involved in many criminal justice issues over the years including their advocacy of alternatives to incarceration, abolition of the death penalty, a moratorium on prison construction, and the establishment of citizen review boards for prisons. The American Friends Service Committee actively opposed the 1991 Omnibus Crime Bill, which advocated the building of new prisons, and in 1990 sponsored its "200 Years of Penitentiary Project," which examined the changing nature of imprisonment since the years of the first prison—which the Quakers themselves built in 1790. The group maintains a Washington, D.C., office for the purpose of sharing their views on peace/justice issues with policy makers. The AFSC has also been active on the issue of AIDS in prisons and health care for inmates. In addition to its criminal justice activities, the AFSC opposes nuclear armament and what it sees as the "militaristic" nature of modern society. The group has been a corecipient of the Nobel Peace Prize.

FURTHER INFORMATION/RESOURCES

The AFSC publishes numerous position papers, pamphlets, and monographs including its *Annual Report* and its semiannual *Quaker Service Bulletin*.

AMERICAN JAIL ASSOCIATION (AJA)
1000 Day Road, Suite 100
Hagerstown, MD 21740
(301) 790–3930

ORGANIZATIONAL HISTORY/DEVELOPMENT

Founded in 1982, American Jail Association (AJA) is a private/nonprofit organization whose membership is primarily composed of corrections officers and administrators. AJA was formed by a merger between two organizations, the National Jail Association (founded 1939) and the National Jail Managers Association (founded 1973). Currently having over 7,000 members and a budget of $1.2 million, AJA sponsors numerous training and accreditation programs for correctional personnel. AJA is affiliated with the American Correctional Association.*

MISSION STATEMENT/PURPOSE

"To band together all those concerned with or interested in the custody and care of persons awaiting trial, serving sentences, or otherwise locally confined; to improve the conditions and systems under which such persons are detained. To advance professionalism through training, information exchange, technical assistance, publications, and conferences. To provide leadership in the development of professional standards, pertinent legislation, management practices, programs and services. To present and advance the interests, needs concerns, and proficiency of the professional as deemed appropriate by the membership and their representatives."

KEY POLICY ACTIVITY/CONCERNS

American Jail Association opposes prison privatization efforts and supports prison-based drug-treatment programs. AJA seeks to establish a "professionalized," credentialed corrections workforce and sponsors educational and practitioner-oriented workshops.

FURTHER INFORMATION/RESOURCES

The AJA publishes *American Jails*, a bimonthly magazine, and *Jail Operations Bulletin*, a monthly newsletter.

AMERICAN JUDGES ASSOCIATION (AJA)
300 Newport Avenue
Williamsburg, VA 23187
(804) 253–2000

ORGANIZATIONAL HISTORY/DEVELOPMENT

Founded in 1983, the American Judges Association (AJA) conducts educational programs for judges and holds an annual educational conference in conjunction with the American Judges Foundation. With over 2,800 members and an annual budget of $100,000, AJA has an active judicial membership. AJA was formerly called the National Association of Municipal Judges (1959) and the North American Judges Association (1972). Since 1972, the organization has gone by its current title.

MISSION STATEMENT/PURPOSE

"To provide professional education and training opportunities to judges. To improve the administration of justice at all levels of the courts and to provide educational opportunities for judges both in formal and informal settings through annual educational conferences and a quality journal."

KEY POLICY ACTIVITY/CONCERNS

Through the establishment of several working committees, AJA actively monitors policy issues in court administration and organization, highway safety, judicial and citizenry education, judicial concerns and standards, and relevant legislation at the federal level. AJA actively supported the overturn of *Pulliam* v. *Allen*, 466 U.S. 522, 529 (1984) which undermined the doctrine of judicial immunity.

FURTHER INFORMATION/RESOURCES

American Jail Association publishes *AJA Benchmark*, a quarterly newsletter, and *Court Review*, a quarterly journal.

AMERICAN JUDICATURE SOCIETY (AJS)
25 E. Washington Street, Suite 1600
Chicago, IL 60611
(312) 558–6900

ORGANIZATIONAL HISTORY/DEVELOPMENT

Founded in 1913 as a private/nonprofit organization, the American Judicature Society (AJS) is made up of attorneys, judges, law professors, government officials, and citizens concerned with justice issues in the United States. Today with over 20,000 members, a full-time staff of twenty, and a budget of over $2.5 million, AJS conducts research, bestows awards, sponsors citizen workshops, and publishes books, studies, and informational pamphlets.

MISSION STATEMENT/PURPOSE

"For the efficient administration of justice."

KEY POLICY ACTIVITY/CONCERNS

Since its inception, AJS has promoted the adoption of "merit plans" for the selection and retention of judges, sponsored numerous citizen conferences on court reform, and been active at both the federal and state levels monitoring judicial/court-oriented policy initiatives. Specifically, AJS assisted in the 1940 adoption of Missouri's "Merit Plan" for choosing judges. During the 1960s and 1970s, AJS sponsored the Citizens Conferences on Court Reform, while during the 1980s and 1990s AJS has increasingly focused its efforts on court education at the local level.

FURTHER INFORMATION/RESOURCES

American Judicature Society began publication of its quarterly journal, *Judicature*, in 1917 and also publishes the *Judicial Conduct Reporter*, a quarterly newsletter.

References

American Judicature Society. (1976). *Indiana Trial Courts: Strategy for Cohesive Change: A Research Project of the American Judicature Society*. Chicago: American Judicature Society.

Korbakes, Chris A. (1978). *Judicial Rulemaking in the State Courts: A Compendium: A Research Project of the American Judicature Society*. Chicago: American Judicature Society.

Osthus, Marlin O. (1980). *State Intermediate Appellate Courts: A Research Project of the American Judicature Society*. Chicago: American Judicature Society.

AMERICAN JUSTICE INSTITUTE (AJI)

Lawrence A. Bennett, President
700 Merchant Street
Sacramento, CA 95814
(916) 442–0707

ORGANIZATIONAL HISTORY/DEVELOPMENT

Formerly the Institute for the Study of Crime and Delinquency (1971), the American Justice Institute (AJI) was established in 1960. In response to a perceived need for a nonprofit, nongovernmental research organization that could bridge the gap between university research and correctional practice, AJI seeks to enhance the use of foundation grants and to improve governmental agency practice. AJI's early focus on grant and contract research, however, has lessened and the institute's resources tend to now be directed toward activities more like those of a foundation. Currently the institute is developing programs that recognize research and achievement, establishes scholarship programs, and supports significant research. The AJI has a seven-member board of directors, a full-time staff of two (which can vary by project), and an annual budget of about $25,000.

MISSION STATEMENT/PURPOSE

"To encourage, sponsor and conduct basic research and surveys; to assemble and disseminate research findings, and to educate its members and the general public with respect to crime and delinquency problems, and their possible solutions."

KEY POLICY ACTIVITY/CONCERNS

The AJI's primary activity is conducting research which it believes is "in service to the correctional community." The AJI has completed numerous research projects including the "International Survey of Corrections," sponsored by the Ford Foundation; the "Correctional Decision Information Project," sponsored by the National Institute of Mental Health; the "Juvenile Drug Offender Project," sponsored by the Rosenberg Foundation; and the "Preston Typology Study," sponsored by the National Institute of Mental Health.

FURTHER INFORMATION/RESOURCES

The AJI makes available copies of its research findings to interested parties and agencies.

Reference

Stapleton, William V. (1982). *Response Strategies to Youth Gang Activity*. Sacramento, CA: American Justice Institute.

AMERICAN PAROLE ASSOCIATION
See National Council on Crime and Delinquency.

AMERICAN PRISON ASSOCIATION
See American Correctional Association.

AMERICAN RESTITUTION ASSOCIATION (ARA)
P.O. Box 154
Shippensburg, PA 17257
(919) 856–5591

ORGANIZATIONAL HISTORY/DEVELOPMENT

Founded in 1981 as a private/nonprofit organization, and formerly known as the National Juvenile Restitution Association (1988), the American Restitution Association (ARA) seeks to promote restitution as a viable alternative to the incarceration of juveniles convicted of property crimes. The ARA currently has over 200 members and an annual budget of about $10,000. In recent years, the ARA has concentrated its efforts on issues of restitution in the criminal justice system generally, rather than exclusively in the juvenile justice system.

MISSION STATEMENT/PURPOSE

"To promote the development of formal restitution/community service programs committed to the practice of accountability building for juvenile and adult offenders."

KEY POLICY ACTIVITY/CONCERNS

While ARA has taken no positions on specific legislation, ARA is generally opposed to the utilization of punitive sanctions (e.g., incarceration) for convicted juveniles and adults. ARA currently cosponsors an annual conference with RESTTA (Restitution Education Specialized Training and Technical Assistance) and has done so since 1988. ARA also conducts workshops, conferences, and provides technical assistance to agencies seeking to institute juvenile and adult restitution programs. Lastly, ARA tends to emphasize the need for victim-oriented programming in the criminal justice system, while simultaneously stressing the need for offender accountability as opposed to simple offender-punishment.

FURTHER INFORMATION/RESOURCES

The ARA publishes a monthly newsletter, *Accountability in Action*, the *Guide to Juvenile Restitution*, and a periodic *Directory of Restitution Programs*.

AMERICANS FOR EFFECTIVE LAW ENFORCEMENT (AELE)
5519 N. Cumberland Avenue #1008
Chicago, IL 60656–1498
(312) 763–2800

ORGANIZATIONAL HISTORY/DEVELOPMENT

Established in 1966 in response to a perceived increase in the national crime problem, Americans for Effective Law Enforcement (AELE) seeks to help police, prosecutors, and the courts promote more effective administration of the criminal law. Over the past several years, AELE has been increasingly involved in providing copies of their amicus curiae briefs to state and national legislators as well as the U.S. Supreme Court. AELE is a nonmembership organization with an average annual budget of over $700,000.

MISSION STATEMENT/PURPOSE

"For the purpose of establishing an organized voice for law-abiding citizens regarding this country's crime problem, and to lend support to professional law enforcement."

KEY POLICY ACTIVITY/CONCERNS

AELE drafts model pieces of legislation designed to assist law enforcement, prosecutors, and courts in the prosecution of criminals. By 1988, AELE had filed amicus curiae ("friend of the court") briefs to the U.S. Supreme Court in 118 separate cases. Twenty-three state attorney generals have signed off on AELE briefs in their respective states. In addition, AELE conducts educational workshops for law enforcement personnel and publishes numerous "position papers" that are distributed widely to members of Congress and state legislators. AELE maintains the Law Enforcement Legal Defense Fund, which provides monies to police officers accused of improper conduct. Lastly, AELE representatives have appeared upon request before legislative committees at all levels of government. In the past, AELE has been opposed to "exclusionary rule" mandates and legislative limits on the scope and breadth of law enforcement activity.

FURTHER INFORMATION/RESOURCES

AELE publishes *Law Enforcement Legal Liability Reporter*, the *Jail and Prisoner Law Bulletin*, and the *Security Legal Update*, each on a monthly basis.

AMERICAN SOCIETY OF CRIMINOLOGY (ASC)
1314 Kinnear Road, Suite 212
Columbus, OH 43212
(614) 292–9207

ORGANIZATIONAL HISTORY/DEVELOPMENT

Founded in 1941, the American Society of Criminology (ASC) is perhaps the premier membership organization for practicing criminologists in the United States. Formerly known as the Society for the Advancement of Criminology (1956), ASC now has over 2,000 members and an annual budget of $150,000.

MISSION STATEMENT/PURPOSE

"To develop criminology as a science and academic discipline; to aid in the construction of criminological curricula at accredited universities; to upgrade the practitioner in criminological fields (e.g. police, prisons, probation, parole, and delinquency)."

KEY POLICY ACTIVITY/CONCERNS

Through the publication of its journal and newsletter, ASC stands as the premier organization in academic criminology. ASC annually bestows numerous awards in the field of criminology, including the Edwin Sutherland Award, the Vollmer Award, and the Sellin-Glueck Award. In addition, ASC coordinates annual conferences in which academic criminological research is presented, discussed, and critiqued.

FURTHER INFORMATION/RESOURCES

ASC publishes *The Criminologist*, a bimonthly newsletter, and *Criminology: An Interdisciplinary Journal*, which comes out quarterly.

AMNESTY INTERNATIONAL USA
John Healy, Executive Director
322 Eighth Avenue
New York, NY 10001
(212) 807–8400

ORGANIZATIONAL HISTORY/DEVELOPMENT

Founded in 1966, Amnesty International works for the humane treatment of prisoners and for the release of political prisoners around the world. The group also adamantly opposes the use of violence and particularly physical and capital punishment. Amnesty International USA currently has over 400,000 members, roughly 1,500 local groups, and a full-time staff of eighty-five.

MISSION STATEMENT/PURPOSE

None provided.

KEY POLICY ACTIVITY/CONCERNS

Widely known for its opposition to the death penalty, Amnesty International most recently entered the criminal justice arena during its 1991 investigation of the Los Angeles County Police and Sheriff's departments' alleged brutality in the Rodney King incident. This videotaped episode of police beating motorist Rodney King with night sticks in the aftermath of a high-speed chase was shown on news broadcasts around the country. The Los Angeles investigation is only the second time Amnesty International USA has investigated allegations of police brutality in this country. The first police brutality investigation took place in Chicago during the early 1980s in which the Chicago police board fired a commander accused of torturing a murder suspect ("Amnesty Team to Investigate Police Brutality Claims," *The Reuter Library Report*, September 22, 1991).

FURTHER INFORMATION/RESOURCES

Amnesty International publishes *Amnesty Action*, a bimonthly newsletter, and *Amnesty International Report*, its annual report. The organization also publishes numerous books, monographs, pamphlets, and position papers on the death penalty and other issues.

References

Amnesty International. (1991). *The Amnesty International Handbook*. Compiled and edited by Marie Staunton, Sally Fenn, and Amnesty International U.S.A. Claremont, CA: Hunter House.
————. (1988). *The Struggle Against Violence and Impunity: A Democratic Commitment: Commentary on an Amnesty International Publication*. Republic of Colombia: Office of the President.
————. (1987). *Political Imprisonment in Cuba: A Special Report From Amnesty International*. Washington, DC: The Cuban-American National Foundation.
————. (1987). *USA the Death Penalty: Amnesty International Briefing*. London: Amnesty International Publications.

ANTI-DEFAMATION LEAGUE OF B'NAI B'RITH (ADL)
823 United Nations Plaza
New York, NY 10017
(212) 490–2525

ORGANIZATIONAL HISTORY/DEVELOPMENT

Founded in 1913 as a private, nonprofit organization devoted to fighting anti-Semitism, the Anti-Defamation League of B'nai B'rith (ADL) has recently been active on the issue of hate crimes and free speech. B'nai B'rith is "the oldest and largest Jewish fraternal organization" and was established in 1843 (Abraham J. Karp, *Haven and Home: A History of the Jews in America* [New York: Schocken Books], p. 345). The ADL currently has a staff of 435 and an annual budget of $35 million.

MISSION STATEMENT/PURPOSE

"To stop the defamation of Jewish people and to secure justice and fair treatment for all citizens alike."

KEY POLICY ACTIVITY/CONCERNS

The ADL has a long history of public activism on behalf of the American Jewish community, however, the organization has most recently been involved in the criminal justice system on issues ranging from inner-city violence to speeches delivered by "hate groups" (see "Hate Laws Scrutinized by Justices: Are Social Goals and the Constitution at Odds?" *The National Law Journal*, December 2, 1991, p. 1). The ADL educates Americans about Israel and maintains the Jewish Foundation for Christian Researchers, the International Center for Holocaust Studies, and its Department of Latin American Affairs. The ADL also bestows four annual awards, the America's Democratic Legacy Award, the Joseph Prize for Human Rights, The Courage to Care Award, and the Hubert H. Humphrey First Amendment Freedom's Prize.

FURTHER INFORMATION/RESOURCES

The ADL publishes numerous books, manuscripts, and pamphlets including the quarterly *Anti-Defamation League Bulletin*, as well as the quarterly publications *Dimensions*, *Face-to-Face Interreligious Bulletin*, and *Middle East Insight*, a journal.

ASSOCIATION FOR CORRECTIONAL RESEARCH AND INFORMATION MANAGERS (ACRIM)
950 Fulton Avenue, Suite 145
Sacramento, CA 95825
(916) 487–9334

ORGANIZATIONAL HISTORY/DEVELOPMENT

Founded in 1961 as a private/nonprofit organization, the Association for Correctional Research and Information Managers (ACRIM) was formerly the Association for Correctional Research and Statistics (1981). Currently the organization has an annual budget of over $50,000 and about one hundred members who are directly involved in correctional research and information management.

MISSION STATEMENT/PURPOSE

"To promote coordination of correctional research among correctional agencies, universities and funding agencies in both the private and governmental sectors."

KEY POLICY ACTIVITY/CONCERNS

ACRIM has been active on the policy front at the state level, taking positions on legislation supporting community-based intermediate punishments as alternatives to incarceration and opposing mandatory sentencing statutes, especially for narcotics offenders. ACRIM applies research data toward the prevention, control, and treatment of crime and delinquency and works to improve research methods in these areas. ACRIM meets annually in conjunction with the American Correctional Association.*

FURTHER INFORMATION/RESOURCES

ACRIM publishes the *ACRIM Newsletter*.

ASSOCIATION FOR CORRECTIONAL RESEARCH AND STATISTICS
See Association for Correctional Research and Information Managers.

ASSOCIATION OF FEDERAL INVESTIGATORS
See Federal Criminal Investigators Association.

ASSOCIATION OF STATE JUVENILE JUSTICE ADMINISTRATORS
See National Association of Juvenile Correctional Agencies.

B
_____ / _____

B'NAI B'RITH, ANTI-DEFAMATION LEAGUE OF
See Anti-Defamation League of B'nai B'rith.

C

——————————————— / ———————————————

CHRISTIAN LEGAL SOCIETY (CLS)
4208 Evergreen Lane, Suite 222
Annandale, VA 22003–3264
(703) 642–1070

ORGANIZATIONAL HISTORY/DEVELOPMENT

Founded in 1961 as a private, nonprofit organization, the Christian Legal Society (CLS) is devoted to providing fellowship, support, and public contact for Christian lawyers and law students. In 1975 CLS founded its Center for Law and Religious Freedom which devotes most of its "activism" time to issues of religious freedom and freedom of expression. CLS describes itself as a "church-state advocacy organization." CLS currently has 4,500 members, a staff of twenty, and an annual budget of $1 million. The group claims members in roughly two-thirds of all accredited law schools in the United States. In 1985, CLS moved its national headquarters to the Washington, D.C., area.

MISSION STATEMENT/PURPOSE

"To equip, inspire and challenge lawyers and law students to serve Jesus Christ through the legal profession."

KEY POLICY ACTIVITY/CONCERNS

The CLS, through its Center for Law and Religious Freedom, provides litigation support, appellate advocacy, and legal expertise on issues ranging from clergy malpractice and taxation of churches to school prayer and other church-state issues. The organization also sponsors reconciliation/mediation programs for the public and seeks to foster the resolution of conflict outside the courts. In addition, CLS sponsors numerous networks and regional associations for law students across the country.

FURTHER INFORMATION/RESOURCES

The CLS publishes a magazine titled *Quarterly*, a monthly newsletter titled *Briefly*, and other quarterly publications titled *Lawyer's Forum* and *Intercessor*.

CHRISTIC INSTITUTE
8773 Venice Blvd.
Los Angeles, CA 90034
(310) 287–1556

ORGANIZATIONAL HISTORY/DEVELOPMENT

Established in 1978, the Christic Institute is a private, nonprofit organization founded by the lawyers and investigators who represented the family of Karen Silkwood in the landmark civil case that expanded protection for citizens against nuclear hazards. The organization is currently well known for its research efforts in the "Iran-Contra" scandal.

MISSION STATEMENT/PURPOSE

Not available.

KEY POLICY ACTIVITY/CONCERNS

Sponsors nationally broadcast teleconference "town meetings" on criminal justice topics, particularly the "drug war."

FURTHER INFORMATION/RESOURCES

No information available.

Reference

Huck, Susan. (1989). *Legal Terrorism: The Truth About the Christic Institute*. New York: New World Publishers.

CITIZENS COMMITTEE FOR THE RIGHT TO KEEP AND BEAR ARMS (CCRKBA)
Liberty Park
12500 NE 10th Place
Bellevue, WA 98005
(206) 454–4911

ORGANIZATIONAL HISTORY/DEVELOPMENT

Established in 1971, and formerly titled the National Citizens Committee for the Right to Keep and Bear Arms (1975), the Citizens Committee for the Right to Keep and Bear Arms (CCRKBA) is one of the strongest anti–gun-control lobbies in the United States. With over 150 current or former members of

Congress serving on its board of advisors, CCRKBA is "wholly devoted to preserving the Second Amendment in its entirely." CCRKBA absorbed the Firearms Lobby of America (1968). With roughly 650,000 members and an annual budget of over $2.5 million, this private/nonprofit organization is second only to the larger National Rifle Association[*] with regard to its advocacy of the Second Amendment.

MISSION STATEMENT/PURPOSE

"To repeal the Gun Control Act of 1968 and to assure that the Second Amendment right of law abiding citizens be preserved. To aggressively mobilize the grass-roots political gun lobby in America to preserve the right to keep and bear arms."

KEY POLICY ACTIVITY/CONCERNS

The Citizens Committee for the Right to Keep and Bear Arms is devoted to securing the right to keep and bear arms as granted under the Second Amendment to the U.S. Constitution. CCRKBA currently holds a national two-day annual policy conference and publishes updates on the policy concerns for members and congressional leaders at the state and national levels. CCRKBA actively supports mandatory sentencing schemes for criminals, especially those convicted of using firearms in the commission of their crimes. In addition, CCRKBA supports a national, point of purchase background check for the purchase of handguns and rifles. CCRKBA has been opposed, however, to a 7-day waiting period on handgun purchases, viewing this as "unnecessarily restrictive." CCRKBA has been an ardent opponent of efforts to place a ban on the importation, manufacture, possession, and sale of semiautomatic military look-alike firearms. Utilizing lobbying, direct mailing, PACs, and grass-roots "phone-tree" mobilization techniques, the CCRKBA is an active and powerful criminal justice policy organization.

FURTHER INFORMATION/RESOURCES

The Citizens Committee for the Right to Keep and Bear Arms publishes *Point Blank*, a monthly newsletter; *Our Vanishing Freedom*, a short manuscript; as well as *The Gun Owner's Political Action Manual* and *The Rights of Gun Owners*.

CITIZENS UNITED FOR THE REHABILITATION OF ERRANTS (CURE)

Charles and Pauline Sullivan
11 15th Street, NE, #6
Washington, DC 20002
(202) 543–8399

ORGANIZATIONAL HISTORY/DEVELOPMENT

Founded in 1972 in Austin, Texas, as a private/nonprofit organization devoted to the opposition of the death penalty, by 1985 Citizens United for the Rehabilitation of Errants (CURE) became a national organization with thirty chapters nationwide. With over 10,000 members and an annual budget of about $30,000, CURE "aims to reduce crime through reform of the criminal justice system."

MISSION STATEMENT/PURPOSE

"To bring about prison reform by organizing families of prisoners, prisoners themselves, and ex-prisoners and concerned citizens. To ensure prisons are used only for those who absolutely must be incarcerated; to ensure prisoners have all the resources they need to turn their lives around."

KEY POLICY ACTIVITY/CONCERNS

CURE lobbies for reform of mandatory sentencing laws at both the state and federal levels, supports the abolition of the death penalty, and enhanced training of law enforcement officials. CURE also emphasizes the importance of family-oriented prison programs for the successful adjustment of inmates in postprison life. CURE opposes restrictions of access to Pell Grants for prisoners and the movement to "privatize" prisons. CURE has worked in conjunction with Amnesty International,* the National Interreligious Task Force, and the Unitarian Universalist Association of Congregations* in its opposition to the death penalty.

FURTHER INFORMATION/RESOURCES

CURE publishes a quarterly national newsletter received by about 5 percent of the members of Congress.

CONFERENCE OF CHIEF JUSTICES (CCJ) (of the National Center for State Courts)

300 Newport Avenue
Williamsburg, VA 23187
(804) 253–2000

ORGANIZATIONAL HISTORY/DEVELOPMENT

Founded in 1949 as a private, nonprofit organization, the Conference of Chief Justices (CCJ) is devoted to the service of the nation's Chief Justices of Supreme Courts of the United States, American Samoa, Guam, Puerto Rico, Mariana Islands, and the Virgin Islands. The CCJ currently has fifty-eight members.

MISSION STATEMENT/PURPOSE

None provided.

KEY POLICY ACTIVITY/CONCERNS

The CCJ was largely responsible for the Bicentennial celebration of the U.S. Constitution in 1976 and is affiliated with the National Center for State Courts.* The organization has published position papers on the issues of judicial restraint versus judicial activism (concerning the degree to which judges should [re] interpret the law) as well as issues of euthanasia and domestic violence. The Conference of Chief Justices also serves as a national clearinghouse on information regarding statutory precedent and issues of federal versus state jurisdiction. In addition, the CCJ has supported efforts which seek to establish "alternative dispute resolution" mediation centers in communities.

FURTHER INFORMATION/RESOURCES

No information available.

CONFLICT RESOLUTION/ALTERNATIVES TO VIOLENCE (CRAV)
William Conway, Director
P.O. Box 256
Rickerhouse
Cherryfield, ME 04622
(207) 546–2780

ORGANIZATIONAL HISTORY/DEVELOPMENT

Founded in 1976 as a private, nonprofit organization made up of a confederation of trained conflict resolution instructors, Conflict Resolution/Alternatives to Violence (CRAV) currently has 200 members. CRAV was formerly the Quaker Center for Prisoner Support Activism (1885).

MISSION STATEMENT/PURPOSE

No formal mission statement.

KEY POLICY ACTIVITY/CONCERNS

CRAV maintains a referral service for interested individuals and organizations and provides trained mediators for the resolution of conflicts in prisons.

FURTHER INFORMATION/RESOURCES

CRAV publishes an informational brochure about its programs and available resources. For more information about the Quakers, see Quaker Committee on Jails and Justice* and the American Friends Service Committee.*

CORRECTIONAL EDUCATION ASSOCIATION (CEA)
8025 Laurel Lakes Court
Laurel, MD 20707
(301) 490–1440

ORGANIZATIONAL HISTORY/DEVELOPMENT

The Correctional Education Association (CEA) was established in 1946 as a private/nonprofit organization devoted to the enhancement of educational skills and the training of correctional staff. The CEA developed as part of a larger movement rooted in the rehabilitative reform efforts of the 1930s. The CEA currently has over 3,200 members and an annual budget of over $150,000. The organization is made up primarily of adult and juvenile education administrators, correctional officers, and adult and juvenile counselors working in federal, state, and county institutions. One of the main functions of the CEA is to facilitate professional contact and networking among correctional professionals.

MISSION STATEMENT/PURPOSE

"To serve educators and administrators who provide services to students in correctional settings. To increase the effectiveness, expertise and skills of members; to create a network of professionals who are leaders in the field of correctional education; to increase the quality of educational programs and services through technical assistance as well as advocacy; to represent the collective interests of correctional education before the government, the press, and the public on the national as well as on the state, provincial and local levels."

KEY POLICY ACTIVITY/CONCERNS

CEA members have been directly involved in special interest group activity in the areas of correctional administration, juvenile education, vocational education, and jail education. CEA published the first list of "Standards for Adult and Juvenile Correctional Educational Programs" and cosponsored the second International Conference of Correctional Educators. In addition, the group hosted two PBS Teleconferences on educational issues in prisons and established the Board of Correctional Education Consultants. CEA bestows annual awards in the field of correctional education and holds an annual conference.

FURTHER INFORMATION/RESOURCES

CEA publishes numerous materials, including a quarterly journal, the *Journal of Correctional Education*, and a quarterly newsletter, *CEA News and Notes*. The group also publishes *Learning Behind Bars: Selected Educational Programs in Prisons*, and *Jails and Juvenile Facilities* with Project Literacy U.S. ("PLUS").

CRIME STOPPERS INTERNATIONAL (CSI)
Tim Kline, Executive Director
3736 Eubank NE, Suite B4
Albuquerque, NM 87111
(505) 294–2300
(800) 245–0009

ORGANIZATIONAL HISTORY/DEVELOPMENT

Crime Stoppers International (CSI) was established in 1976 as a private/ nonprofit organization designed to combat neighborhood crime by organizing community efforts at crime awareness in Albuquerque, New Mexico. Formerly titled Crime Stoppers USA (1984), Crime Stoppers International conducts workshops and presentations oriented toward raising community awareness and interaction with law enforcement. With over 700 local programs divided into ten regional groups, CSI offers cash awards for information leading to the resolution of crimes in communities nationwide.

MISSION STATEMENT/PURPOSE

"CSI endeavors to facilitate the establishment of Crime Stoppers programs across the country, to provide workshops and training for interested citizens' groups, and to contribute to the apprehension of criminals and the reduction of crime generally."

KEY POLICY ACTIVITY/CONCERNS

Members of Crime Stoppers International have become active participants in debates about many criminal justice issues, including due process and proper criminal procedure, particularly with regard to the establishment of "probable cause" and "illegal search and seizure" issues. In *U.S.* v. *Zamora*, 784 F.2d 1025 (10th Cir. 1986), for example, the Tenth Circuit of the United States Court of Appeals ruled that a Crime Stoppers informant's name need not be revealed during the prosecution of a criminal case. In another relevant case (not involving a member of Crime Stoppers), the U.S. Supreme Court ruled, in *Alabama* v. *White,* 496 U.S. (1990), that a less demanding standard of "reasonable suspicion of criminal activity" may be utilized instead of the more stringent requirements of "probable cause" at times when law enforcement receives information from an anonymous source. This decision involved a case where an anonymous informant had provided police with information about a potential drug dealer's possession of controlled substances in her car. Using information from an anonymous source, police stopped the driver, questioned her, and obtained verbal permission to search the car. The defendant in this case later argued that police must first attempt to "sufficiently corroborate" anonymous information before "probable cause" may be established. In this 6 to 3 ruling, the U.S. Supreme Court affirmed the use of anonymous informants by law enforcement as a viable method of building criminal cases (Judge Walter W. Carter, CSI Legal Counsel, "Victory for Crime Stoppers," *The Caller*, June 1990, pp. 2, 10). CSI's most prominent activity, however, consists of assisting in the nationwide broadcast of reenactments of crimes on nationally syndicated television shows. The group also assists law enforcement organizations in disseminating information and bulletins via public service announcements, conducting workshops, and offering awards for citizen "crime stoppers." CSI also holds an annual conference.

FURTHER INFORMATION/RESOURCES

CSI publishes *The Caller*, a monthly magazine, and a *Directory* of CSI programs annually.

CRIME STOPPERS, USA
See Crime Stoppers International.

D

/

DEATH ROW SUPPORT PROJECT (DRSP)
Rachel Gross, Coordinator
P.O. Box 600
Liberty Mills, IN 46946
(219) 982–7480

ORGANIZATIONAL HISTORY/DEVELOPMENT

The Death Row Support Project (DRSP) was founded in 1978 as a private/ nonprofit organization which seeks to facilitate communication between interested correspondents and death row inmates across the country. One significant event in the life of the organization occurred when a correspondent was asked to witness the execution of the inmate with whom he had been writing. The correspondent later wrote an opinion-editor piece, published in the *Washington Post*, prompting a national debate on execution ("The Execution of Ronnie Dunkins," *Washington Post*, July 22, 1989, p. A23). Currently DRSP has over 1,200 participants and is funded in large part by the Church of the Brethren and individual correspondents.

MISSION STATEMENT/PURPOSE

"To provide support for persons under sentence of death in the U.S. and to educate the general public about the death penalty through the experience of writing to someone on death row."

KEY POLICY ACTIVITY/CONCERNS

While the Death Row Support Project has not lobbied nor taken formal positions on policy, the group promotes the abolition of the death penalty.

FURTHER INFORMATION/RESOURCES

Those interested in corresponding with inmates under sentence of death via the DRSP may obtain the names and addresses of such prisoners by writing to the above address.

DRUG POLICY FOUNDATION (DPF)
4801 Massachusetts Avenue, NW
Suite 400
Washington, DC 20016
(202) 895–1634

ORGANIZATIONAL HISTORY/DEVELOPMENT

Established in 1987 as a private/nonprofit organization comprised of academics, corporate executives, and private citizens from numerous countries, the Drug Policy Foundation (DPF) seeks to promote the view of the "drug problem" as a medical policy question rather than a criminal justice or enforcement issue. Today, with a full-time staff of fourteen and a membership of over 5,000, the DPF opposes the "zero tolerance" policies of the current "drug war" and promotes alternatives such as legalization of marijuana, decriminalization of possession of controlled substances, and specifically the "medicalization" of marijuana and heroin.

MISSION STATEMENT/PURPOSE

"To provide leadership in the public debate on drugs by presenting accurate facts and alternative policies, including legislation, decriminalization and medicalization."

KEY POLICY ACTIVITY/CONCERNS

The DPF has actively supported the legalization of marijuana, the establishment of needle exchange programs in inner cities, and the permissible possession of small amounts of marijuana for personal use (i.e., decriminalization). The DPF has been opposed to policies advocating random or mandatory mass urine testing due to the high rate of "false positive" test results. Through lobbying and direct mail, the DPF has advocated legalization of medicinal uses of marijuana and the implementation of needle exchange programs. DPF, however, has also been generally supportive of "police action against predatory drug traffickers." For example, the group promoted certain facets of the Omnibus Crime Bill of 1991, which asserted that the criminalization of drug use has increased the incidence of violence against police officers.

FURTHER INFORMATION/RESOURCES

The DPF sponsors several forums, conferences, and seminars—many taking place on Capitol Hill ''in order to provide Congressional staff and the national media with expert advice on alternative drug control policies.'' DPF publishes a quarterly newsletter and numerous books and pamphlets which may be obtained at the above address.

F

———————————— / ————————————

FEDERAL CRIMINAL INVESTIGATORS ASSOCIATION (FCIA)

Ernst J. Alexander, President
P.O. Box 1256
Detroit, MI 48231
(512) 229–5601

ORGANIZATIONAL HISTORY/DEVELOPMENT

Established in 1953 as a private/nonprofit organization designed to improve and promote the profession of federal law enforcement, the Federal Criminal Investigators Association (FCIA) now has over 5,000 members and an annual budget exceeding $100,000. Formerly the U.S. Treasury Agents Association (1968), the FCIA has membership committees established for monitoring legislation, establishing scholarships, and conducting seminars and workshops. The FCIA merged with the Association of Federal Investigators in 1991.

MISSION STATEMENT/PURPOSE

"To recognize and promote the profession of federal law enforcement."

KEY POLICY ACTIVITY/CONCERNS

The FCIA participates in lobbying and in direct mailing on numerous criminal justice policies at the federal level. The FCIA impacted the establishment of the presidential Cabinet position of "Drug Czar" and the creation of the National Law Enforcement Memorial. In addition, the FCIA makes funds available to the families of law enforcement officers killed in the line of duty and maintains the Missing Children's Hotline. The FCIA actively testified before Congress in support of the enforcement provisions of the Omnibus Crime Bill of 1991. The group also conducts telephone campaigns, training seminars, and annual award and scholarship ceremonies.

FURTHER INFORMATION/RESOURCES

The FCIA publishes the *Federal Criminal Investigator*, a quarterly magazine, and *The Pro-Gram*, a monthly newsletter. FCIA also holds an annual convention.

THE FIREARMS LOBBY
See Citizens Committee for the Right to Keep and Bear Arms.

FORTUNE SOCIETY (FS)
JoAnne Page, Executive Director
39 W. 19th Street, 7th Floor
New York, NY 10011
(212) 206–7070

ORGANIZATIONAL HISTORY/DEVELOPMENT

Founded in 1967 as a private, nonprofit organization devoted to educating the public about criminal justice issues, the Fortune Society (FS) is active in helping both offenders released from prison and "high-risk" youth. The FS currently has over 9,000 members and a staff of fifty-five. The organization's annual budget now exceeds $2 million. The primary activities of FS are counseling, education, career development, court advocacy, and outpatient substance abuse treatment services. The Fortune Society is one of the largest prisoner advocacy groups in the country.

MISSION STATEMENT/PURPOSE

"To educate the public about prisons, criminal justice issues, and the root causes of crime and, through education and counseling, help ex-offenders and young people break the cycle of repeated crime and incarceration. What makes Fortune Society uniquely effective is that its counselors and many of its staff are ex-offenders themselves: men and women who have changed their own lives, and who serve as powerful role models for their clients. We at Fortune believe that every human being has the ability to change, even in the face of enormous obstacles. We are committed to helping offenders break patterns of behavior that are destructive to themselves, to their families, and to the community. When they succeed, everyone gains. At Fortune we are committed to human change, one life at a time."

KEY POLICY ACTIVITY/CONCERNS

Fortune Society is perhaps best known for its programs in which ex-offenders go into the public schools, and on television, to share their prison experiences with the public and to educate children about the "cost" of crime. The Fortune Society has also recently offered AIDS counseling to inmates. In 1973 the FS established its first tutoring program for ex-offenders; in 1974 its first career development program; in 1980 its Court Advocacy program; and in 1991 FS began providing AIDS-related services to inmates. The organization also recently started a drug treatment (outpatient) program for ex-offenders.

FURTHER INFORMATION/RESOURCES

The Fortune Society publishes a quarterly newspaper titled *Fortune News*, which is distributed free to inmates and sponsors of the society.

FRATERNAL ORDER OF POLICE (FOP)
Dewey R. Stokes, National President
National Headquarters FOP
2100 Gardiner Lane
Louisville, KY 40205–2900
(800) 451–2711

ORGANIZATIONAL HISTORY/DEVELOPMENT

Founded in 1915 as the Grand Lodge Fraternal Order of Police, the Fraternal Order of Police (FOP) is the nation's largest law enforcement organization and acts much like a large police officers' union. With over 230,000 members, an annual budget of over $1 million, and some 1,900 "lodges" across the country, the FOP is active in a number of issues related to the law enforcement profession—particularly with regard to wages, benefits, and pension concerns. FOP involvement, however, ranges from issues in police/public relations and benefits for police officers to monitoring national, state, and local initiatives that affect law enforcement. The organization sees itself as the "voice of the working police officers of this country."

MISSION STATEMENT/PURPOSE

"To improve the profession of law enforcement by improving working conditions, wages and benefits, and by monitoring legislation affecting law enforcement on the local, state, and national levels."

KEY POLICY ACTIVITY/CONCERNS

The FOP is an active criminal justice organization, providing amicus curiae briefs to the U.S. Supreme Court and testifying before legislative hearings in addition to participating in the drafting of legislative language. Some examples of initiatives which the FOP has supported in the past include: the Public Safety Officers' Benefits Act of 1976; the National Peace Officers Memorial Resolution; legislation banning the manufacture, sale, and importation of armor-piercing ammunition; the Omnibus Anti-Drug Legislation Act of 1988; a waiting period on handgun purchases; and legislation that facilitates the use of assets seized in criminal activity by law enforcement. The FOP has been opposed to the "exclusionary rule" and other measures which, in their view, "restrain" law enforcement.

FURTHER INFORMATION/RESOURCES

The FOP publishes numerous booklets, pamphlets, and informational leaflets. *The Journal* is a quarterly periodical of the FOP.

FRIENDS OUTSIDE
Judy Evans, Executive Director
2105 Hamilton Avenue, Suite 290
San Jose, CA 95125
(408) 879–0691

ORGANIZATIONAL HISTORY/DEVELOPMENT

Established in 1955 as a private/nonprofit, nonmembership organization, Friends Outside has become one of the largest prisoner advocacy groups in the country. With a staff of about ninety, sixteen local working groups, and an annual budget of over $2.5 million, Friends Outside seeks to provide programs and services to adult prisoners and their families. Friends Outside became the first private organization ever granted office space inside a state prison and is currently maintaining nineteen such offices in the California prison system.

MISSION STATEMENT/PURPOSE

"To assist families, prisoners, and ex-prisoners with the immediate and long term effects of incarceration and to act as a bridge between those we serve, the community at large and the criminal justice system, thereby enhancing the character of justice."

KEY POLICY ACTIVITY/CONCERNS

Friends Outside deals mainly with parole violators in the California corrections system. Friends Outside has sponsored work-furlough programs for parolees in the California prison system and stresses self-reliance to prisoners as they reenter society upon release. Friends Outside promotes several family and community-support oriented prisoners programs for inmates and parolees. Since 1979 the program has expanded by establishing itself in the Nevada Department of Corrections in both minimum and maximum security jails and prisons. Much of the group's time is devoted to maintaining support groups for adult inmates and juveniles and their families. Friends Outside engages in no direct lobbying activity.

FURTHER INFORMATION/RESOURCES

Friends Outside publishes a monthly newsletter, *Friends Outside*.

G

/

GOVERNOR'S CONFERENCE
See National Governor's Association.

GRAND LODGE FRATERNAL ORDER OF POLICE
See Fraternal Order of Police.

GUARDIAN ANGELS
982 E. 89th Street
Brooklyn, NY 11236
(212) 420–1324

ORGANIZATIONAL HISTORY/DEVELOPMENT

Established in 1979 and formerly called the "Magnificent 13," the controversial Guardian Angels formed as a coalition of unarmed citizens who voluntarily patrolled public areas in New York and (later) other major cities across the United States. With the goal of deterring crime by utilizing powers of "citizen's arrest" and projecting an ominous presence, Guardian Angels' members patrol public areas wearing their trademark white T-shirts and red berets. The group has expanded their program to some fifty cities across the United States and today claims over 5,000 members. The Guardian Angels sponsor self-defense courses, provide "crime awareness" training, and hold an annual conference.

MISSION STATEMENT/PURPOSE

"To provide positive role models for young people by patrolling subways, buses, streets, ferries, and multiple dwellings."

KEY POLICY ACTIVITY/CONCERNS

The Guardian Angels' main concern is the deterrence of crime through practices of citizen's arrest and high-profile dress. The group engages in no formal lobbying, but nevertheless has maintained an active public presence on venues such as television interview programs. The Guardian Angels have received mixed reviews from communities wherever they've gone—with once Philadelphia police chief (now Los Angeles) Willie Williams, for example, expressing concern over the group's rough tactics of "citizen's arrest."

FURTHER INFORMATION/RESOURCES

No information available.

H

---- / ----

HANDGUN CONTROL, INC. (HCI)
1225 I Street, NW, Suite 1100
Washington, DC 20005
(202) 898–0792

ORGANIZATIONAL HISTORY/DEVELOPMENT

Founded in 1974 as a private, nonprofit organization devoted to the legislative control of handgun ownership, Handgun Control, Inc. (HCI) was formerly titled the National Council to Control Handguns. HCI currently has over 250,000 members and an annual budget of close to $7 million.

MISSION STATEMENT/PURPOSE

Not available.

KEY POLICY ACTIVITY/CONCERNS

HCI lobbies Congress and activates citizens toward the establishment of legislatively mandated controls on the purchase and ownership of handguns in the United States. The organization also seeks to establish restrictions on the manufacture and sale of firearms in the United States. HCI maintains statistics on the comparatively high American rate of death caused by handguns and, in its literature, compares these statistics to that of other countries.

FURTHER INFORMATION/RESOURCES

HCI publishes the quarterly *Handgun Control—Washington Report*, and has published the influential book *Guns Don't Die—People Do*. The organization also periodically publishes legislative "Action Guides" and has produced a documentary video on handgun violence in the United States.

I

---- / ----

INSTITUTE FOR THE STUDY OF DELINQUENCY
See American Justice Institute.

**INTERNATIONAL ASSOCIATION FOR THE STUDY OF
ORGANIZED CRIME (IASOC)**
Department of Criminal Justice
C.W. Post Campus
Long Island University
Brookville, NY 11548
(516) 299–2594

ORGANIZATIONAL HISTORY/DEVELOPMENT

Founded in 1984 as a private/nonprofit organization consisting primarily of researchers, professors, and students, the International Association for the Study of Organized Crime (IASOC) was established to facilitate the dissemination of information on organized crime to interested parties. In 1985 the IASOC was recognized by then President Reagan and today has over 400 members in nine different countries.

MISSION STATEMENT/PURPOSE

"To promote the communication and dissemination of information among members, other associations, and criminal justice agencies. To encourage limited and long-range research into organized crime. To establish a vehicle capable of providing research and evaluative services to public and private agencies. To establish a center for the accumulation and dissemination of information for courses on organized crime and related subjects."

KEY POLICY ACTIVITY/CONCERNS

The IASOC is regarded internationally as an authority on organized crime activity, recently being cited, for example, in a *U.S. News & World Report* cover story (March 4, 1991, p. 13) on the brutal tactics of the Sicilian Mafia during Italy's recent rash of suspected Mafia-related killings. The organization holds annual meetings in conference with the American Society of Criminology.* In 1988, IASOC sponsored its first international conference.

FURTHER INFORMATION/RESOURCES

In 1985 IASOC began to publish a newsletter, *Update*, which in 1988 was retitled *Criminal Organizations*.

INTERNATIONAL ASSOCIATION OF CHIEFS OF POLICE (IACP)

1110 N. Glebe Road, Suite 200
Arlington, VA 22201
(703) 836–6767

ORGANIZATIONAL HISTORY/DEVELOPMENT

Founded in 1893 as the National Chiefs of Police Union, the International Association of Chiefs of Police (IACP) is one of the oldest police organizations in the country. In the early 1900s a national movement developed in which the "professionalization" of the law enforcement field and of police officers in general was promoted in the interest of controlling police corruption. During the first two decades of the twentieth century, the IACP became the leading voice for police reform (Joseph J. Senna and Larry J. Siegel, *Introduction to Criminal Justice* [New York: West Publishing Co., 1984], p. 149). The IACP currently has 14,000 members, an annual budget of about $1 million, and a full-time staff of sixty-two.

MISSION STATEMENT/PURPOSE

Not available.

KEY POLICY ACTIVITY/CONCERNS

Comprised principally of law enforcement executives, the IACP deals primarily with issues of police professionalization at an international level. The IACP encourages cross-cultural comparison of law enforcement training methods and promotes training in law enforcement management techniques for police executives. The IACP has been heavily involved in the establishment of police academy training standards and has assisted in the development of training programs. The IACP sponsors research into methods used in training academies and particularly on police resource-management techniques.

FURTHER INFORMATION/RESOURCES

The IACP publishes numerous informational pamphlets and monographs, including *Police Chief: The Professional View of Law Enforcement*, a monthly magazine, and the annual *Directory of IACP Members*.

INTERNATIONAL ASSOCIATION OF POLICE PROFESSORS
See Academy of Criminal Justice Sciences.

INTERNATIONAL ASSOCIATION OF RESIDENTIAL AND COMMUNITY ALTERNATIVES (IARCA)
Paul Kinsiger, Administrator
P.O. Box 7051
Marquette, MI 49855
(608) 785–0200

ORGANIZATIONAL HISTORY/DEVELOPMENT

Founded in 1964 as the International Halfway House Association, the International Association of Residential and Community Alternatives (IARCA) currently sponsors over 1,500 programs across the country devoted to "establishing community-based treatment programs for the socially stigmatized." Focusing its efforts in the areas of mental health, substance abuse, and corrections, IARCA has over 1,000 members and an annual budget of $250,000.

MISSION STATEMENT/PURPOSE

None provided.

KEY POLICY ACTIVITY/CONCERNS

With 260 agencies representing over 1,500 IARCA programs, IARCA assists members in the exchange of information relating to the management and treatment of mental health patients, inmates, and substance-addicted persons. The organization has taken no explicit positions on legislation in recent years, however, it has participated in direct mailing and public education campaigns in support of community-based treatment.

FURTHER INFORMATION/RESOURCES

The IARCA publishes a *Directory of Residential Treatment Centers*, biennially, the *IARCA Journal*, bimonthly, and a number of different topical newsletters. The group also sponsors a semiannual conference and a biennial international conference.

INTERNATIONAL HALFWAY HOUSE ASSOCIATION
See International Association of Residential and Community Alternatives.

INTERNATIONAL PRISON MINISTRY (IPM)

Chaplain Ray Hoekstra, Director
P.O. Box 63
Dallas, TX 75221
(214) 494–2302
(800) 527–1212

ORGANIZATIONAL HISTORY/DEVELOPMENT

Founded in 1969 as a private, nonprofit organization devoted to the rehabilitation of criminals through Christian conversion, the International Prison Ministry (IPM) has grown to be one of the nation's leading jail volunteer organizations.

MISSION STATEMENT/PURPOSE

"To rehabilitate prisoners through the process of Christian Conversion and discipleship."

KEY POLICY ACTIVITY/CONCERNS

The IPM conducts "revivals" in many Texas prisons and broadcasts religious radio and television programs aimed especially at prisoners. Recently, the organization has assisted in the distribution of over 100,000 bibles to prisoners in the former Soviet Union.

FURTHER INFORMATION/RESOURCES

The International Prison Ministry publishes *Prison Evangelism Magazine*, quarterly, in addition to numerous books and pamphlets devoted to prisoners. The IPM holds an annual conference in conjunction with the American Correctional Chaplain's Association.

J

———————— / ————————

JOHN HOWARD ASSOCIATION (JHA)
Michael J. Mahoney, Executive Director
67 E. Madison, Suite 1416
Chicago, IL 60603
(312) 263–1901

ORGANIZATIONAL HISTORY/DEVELOPMENT

The John Howard Association (JHA) was established in 1901 as a private, nonprofit, nonsectarian organization named after the eighteenth-century English prison reformer John Howard (1726–1790). The group concerns itself with the spiritual well-being of prisoners and the establishment of alternatives to incarceration. The group currently has about 250 members, a full-time staff of five, and an annual budget of $350,000.

MISSION STATEMENT/PURPOSE

"To bring about fair and effective correctional programs that are responsive to the needs of both offenders and the general community. To promote fair and effective prisons and jails, sentencing policies, and promote fair and effective nonincarcerative options."

KEY POLICY ACTIVITY/CONCERNS

The John Howard Association actively lobbies for correctional and court reform at the state and local level, provides research and survey services in the field of criminal justice, and periodically issues policy statements on criminal justice issues. The organization also acts as a "watchdog agency" through the creation of its "Illinois Prisons and Jails Project," in which JHA representatives visit the Cook County Jail once per week and make periodic visits to Illinois' other prisons and juvenile facilities throughout the year. The JHA receives over

2,000 requests for information and assistance per year from prisoners incarcerated in Illinois prisons and jails. In addition, the group sponsors public education campaigns and maintains a speaker's bureau. Recently, JHA representatives became court-appointed monitors in numerous consent decrees involving over-crowding in Illinois prisons and jails. In addition, the group recently lobbied in support of Illinois legislation promoting ''good time'' release for inmates completing academic or vocational programs while incarcerated. With a long history of criminal justice activity dating back to the organization's promotion of a public defender's office in Cook County, Illinois, in 1916, this group is a widely recognized criminal justice advocacy group.

FURTHER INFORMATION/RESOURCES

The John Howard Association publishes a newsletter, *UPDATE*, and numerous other pamphlets, research reports, and position papers.

THE *JOURNAL OF PRISONERS ON PRISONS*
Howard Davidson, Editor
P.O. Box 779, R.P.O. 11
Edmonton, Alberta T6G 2EO
CANADA

ORGANIZATIONAL HISTORY/DEVELOPMENT

Founded in 1988 by a group of Canadian inmates, the *Journal of Prisoners on Prisons* has broadened its repertoire to include articles from inmates confined in American prisons and jails. Originally published twice per year, the journal is now published quarterly.

MISSION STATEMENT/PURPOSE

''The *Journal of Prisoners on Prisons* is the only existing refereed academic journal devoted to criminal justice/corrections issues in which prisoners themselves are the primary authors.''

KEY POLICY ACTIVITY/CONCERNS

The *Journal of Prisoners on Prisons* provides an academic forum through which incarcerated persons in Canada and the United States may discuss issues relevant to incarceration while remaining grounded in the realities of prison life via the experiences of prisoners themselves. The *Journal* has published papers on the use of hashish by imprisoned Native Americans for religious purposes, the goals and abuses of ''rehabilitation'' efforts in prisons, prison overcrowding, and numerous other corrections-related research topics.

FURTHER INFORMATION/RESOURCES

The *Journal of Prisoners on Prisons* is published quarterly.

**JUDICIAL PROCESS COMMISSION (JPC) (of the Greater
Rochester Community of Churches)**
121 North Fitzhugh Street
Rochester, NY 14614
(716) 325–7727

ORGANIZATIONAL HISTORY/DEVELOPMENT

Founded in 1972 as a private, nonprofit organization in response to an incident
of police brutality in Rochester, New York, and the Attica Prison riot, the Judicial
Process Commission (JPC) of the Greater Rochester Community of Churches is
one of the most active and engaged criminal justice reform groups in the country.
Since its inception the group has focused its attention on community conflict
resolution, the creation of reconciliation task forces, and alternatives to incarceration. The JPC currently has a part-time staff of three and an annual budget
of $50,000.

MISSION STATEMENT/PURPOSE

"JPC challenges society to create a just, non-violent community which em-
powers all people to reach their highest potential. We do this through education,
conflict resolution training and advocacy for change in the justice system. These
changes can be achieved only through addressing the basic inequities in our
society."

KEY POLICY ACTIVITY/CONCERNS

With a long history of criminal justice activism, the JPC has engaged in
numerous activities including: the formation of the New York State Coalition
on Criminal Justice, an ecumenical coalition of churches which seeks "to educate
the state legislature on justice issues" (1974); establishing the Creative Options
in New Sentencing coalition, which monitors Monroe County (Rochester area)
criminal justice initiatives (1982); publishing a position paper on police mis-
conduct and establishing a funding base for victims of police brutality to litigate
(1984); participating in the Rochester Coalition Against the Death Penalty (1988);
and convening the Rochester Public Safety and Civil Rights Coalition toward
the establishment of a police civilian review board (1990).

The JPC also conducts conflict resolution training seminars in schools and
congregations and for the general public. In addition, the organization engages
in educational and advocacy work for the establishment of alternatives to incarceration, sponsors victim offender reconciliation programs in the Rochester
area, and has assisted the Rochester Police Department in the establishment of
a community relations training requirement for Rochester police officers. In the
past the group has been generally opposed to prison expansion initiatives, the
death penalty, and habitual offender statutes.

FURTHER INFORMATION/RESOURCES

The JPC publishes *Justicia*, a quarterly newsletter, and numerous other research and position papers, including "The Genesee Conciliator" (a bimonthly newsletter), the "Position Paper on Deadly Force," "Crime and Community and Biblical Perspective," and "Restorative Justice: Toward Nonviolence."

JUDICIAL SELECTION PROJECT (JSP)
Nan Aron, Executive Director
c/o Alliance for Justice
1601 Connecticut Avenue, NW, Suite 600
Washington, DC 20009
(202) 332–3224

ORGANIZATIONAL HISTORY/DEVELOPMENT

Founded in 1968 as a private, nonprofit organization by the Alliance for Justice, the Judicial Selection Project (JSP) seeks to ensure the existence of a competent and independent judiciary at the federal level. The organization has been particularly active in recent years in response to the comparatively large number of federal judicial posts filled by the appointments of the Reagan and Bush administrations.

MISSION STATEMENT/PURPOSE

Not available.

KEY POLICY ACTIVITY/CONCERNS

The JSP monitors all judicial appointments made by the executive branch and investigates the judicial and personal records of all such appointees. The JSP is viewed as being progressive in its persuasion and has been particularly sensitive to issues of civil rights and judicial activism (where judges offer their own [re] interpretation of constitutional mandates). The Judicial Selection Project is certainly one of the most energetic interest groups with regard to the federal judiciary and has had a substantial voice in the media. The Judicial Selection Project most recently opposed the nomination of Clarence Thomas to the U.S. Supreme Court.

FURTHER INFORMATION/RESOURCES

The JSP makes frequent statements to the media on various issues relevant to the federal judiciary, most often regarding a particular appointee's qualifications (or lack thereof) for a specific judicial post.

JUSTICE FELLOWSHIP (JF) (An affiliate of PRISON FELLOWSHIP MINISTRIES)
P.O. Box 17181
Washington, DC 20041–0181
(800) 787–5245
(703) 834–3650

ORGANIZATIONAL HISTORY/DEVELOPMENT

Founded in 1983, Justice Fellowship (JF) is the criminal justice reform arm of Prison Fellowship Ministries. Since its inception, Justice Fellowship has placed increasing emphasis on resolving conflicts outside of the criminal justice system via reconciliation programs and community-based alternatives to incarceration. Justice Fellowship is now considered by many to be the leading "religiously based" criminal justice interest group in the country. Justice Fellowship currently has twenty-three active state task forces nationwide that monitor criminal justice legislation and actively participate in the drafting of legislation.

MISSION STATEMENT/PURPOSE

"To promote Biblical standards of justice in the American criminal justice system. To assist government officials to implement restorative justice programs and which establish rights for victims to participate in the criminal justice system."

KEY POLICY ACTIVITY/CONCERNS

JF takes positions on criminal justice legislation at both the state and national levels, particularly those directed at establishing community corrections programs, victim offender reconciliation programs (see PACT Institute of Justice*), and victims' rights legislation. In literature published by Justice Fellowship, the organization states that it has "three primary national criminal justice objectives." They are: "(1) To significantly increase the number of intermediate sanction programs available to non-dangerous offenders; (2) to significantly expand the number of incarcerated offenders working in prison industry programs that teach usable job skills and pay fair wages; (3) to significantly increase the participation of crime victims in all stages of the criminal justice process and to expand the use of restitution as a punishment option for offenders."

At the national level, JF representatives testified before Congress during the drafting stages of the 1990 Omnibus Crime Bill. Justice Fellowship has opposed harsh mandatory sentencing schemes in favor of "community punishment" options, particularly restitution programs. The group also raises and contributes substantial sums of money for community corrections programs.

The central activity of Prison Fellowship, however, is in the training and sponsorship of individuals in prison ministry and fellowship programs. Prison Fellowship sponsors workshops, Bible classes, family/marriage counseling, and correspondence and visitation programs in prisons. Prison Fellowship is affiliated with the American Correctional Association.*

FURTHER INFORMATION/RESOURCES

Justice Fellowship publishes *The Justice Report*, a quarterly newsletter, and numerous pamphlets and books, including *Beyond Crime and Punishment: Restorative Justice* and *Is There a Better Way?: A Case for Alternatives to Prison*. Prison Fellowship has published *Convicted: New Hope for Ending America's Crime Crisis*, *Life Sentence*, and numerous other position papers and pamphlets.

K

KERNER COMMISSION
See Milton S. Eisenhower Foundation.

L

LAMBDA ALPHA EPSILON
See American Criminal Justice Association.

M

––––––––––––––––––––– / –––––––––––––––––––––

"MAGNIFICENT 13"
See Guardian Angels.

MENNONITE CENTRAL COMMITTEE (MCC)
21 S. 12th Street
P.O. Box 500
Akron, PA 17501–0500
(717) 859–1151

ORGANIZATIONAL HISTORY/DEVELOPMENT

Founded in 1920 as the service agency of the North American Mennonite and Brethren in Christ churches, the Mennonite Central Committee (MCC) is active in many criminal justice issues. Particularly active in victim's rights, restitution, and reconciliation between victim and offender, the MCC is among the most active of religiously based criminal justice interest groups. Currently the organization is divided into nine regional groups across the country and has an annual budget of close to $30 million.

MISSION STATEMENT/PURPOSE

None provided.

KEY POLICY ACTIVITY/CONCERNS

The Mennonite Central Committee has been influential in developing Victim-Offender Reconciliation Programs ("VORPs") across the country as well as in promoting alternatives to incarceration. The MCC has been supportive of conscientious objectors during times of war and has worked closely with other religious groups on a spectrum of criminal justice and political issues (see American Friends Service Committee* and Quaker Committee on Jails and Justice*).Mennonites are widely known for their avowed pacifism. (For more information on "VORP" programs, see separate entry for PACT Institute of Justice.*)

FURTHER INFORMATION/RESOURCES

The MCC publishes the *Mennonite Central Committee—Network Newsletter*, which deals with criminal justice issues; the *Conciliation Quarterly*; the *Draft Counselor's Update*; and numerous other books, monographs, and pamphlets.

MILTON S. EISENHOWER FOUNDATION (MSEF)
1725 I Street, NW, Suite 504
Washington, DC 20006
(202) 429–0440

ORGANIZATIONAL HISTORY/DEVELOPMENT

Established in 1981 as a private, nonprofit organization founded to continue the work of the earlier Eisenhower and Kerner Commissions on the Causes and Prevention of Violence (established after the urban violence of the mid-1960s), the Milton S. Eisenhower Foundation (MSEF) sponsors urban programs designed to keep youths constructively occupied. The MSEF is one of the largest private criminal justice foundations, with an annual budget of $2 million. The organization's namesake, Milton S. Eisenhower, was the brother of the late President Eisenhower.

MISSION STATEMENT/PURPOSE

None available.

KEY POLICY ACTIVITY/CONCERNS

The MSEF is devoted to "addressing the deterioration in our inner cities" by providing resources and technical assistance to community development programs in urban areas. The MSEF has sponsored numerous programs providing youth with job training, counseling, recreation facilities, "big brothers," tutoring, and other community support. Specializing in the sponsorship of comparatively small programs, the MSEF has been quite successful in its efforts to combat teenage pregnancy, family violence, and school dropout rates. The organization also sponsors "exchange programs" with Great Britain, China, the (former) Soviet Union, and Japan. In late 1990, the MSEF recommended in its corporate-sponsored tenth anniversary report that $10 billion be devoted to the reconstruction of the inner cities, a suggestion that was later rejected by the Bush administration.

FURTHER INFORMATION/RESOURCES

The MSEF publishes an annual report and regular *Commission Updates.*

MOTHERS AGAINST DRUNK DRIVING (MADD)
Robert J. King, Executive Director
511 John Carpenter Freeway, Number 700
Irving, TX 75062
(214) 744–6233

ORGANIZATIONAL HISTORY/DEVELOPMENT

Founded in 1980 as a private, nonprofit organization designed to promote public awareness about drunk driving, Mothers Against Drunk Driving (MADD) is one of the largest private interest groups in the United States. Focusing much of its attention on victim assistance, the organization currently has close to 3 million members, a staff of 262, and an annual budget of close to $40 million.

MISSION STATEMENT/PURPOSE

"The mission of Mothers Against Drunk Driving is to stop drunk driving and to support victims of this violent crime."

KEY POLICY ACTIVITY/CONCERNS

MADD has supported law enforcement's use of mandatory roadblock checkpoints, mandatory seat belt laws, and the use of breath tests. The group has also been extremely influential in the passage of enhanced punishments for those convicted of drunk driving. MADD representatives testify before Congress, provide statistical information to legislative committees, serve on drunk driving task forces throughout the country, and monitor state and local courts for drunk driving penalties. The organization currently has affiliates in forty-eight states. A large percentage of the organization's resources are devoted to assisting victims and loved ones of those injured or killed in accidents involving drunk driving. Along these lines, MADD has established a Victims Assistance Outreach Program, which assists victims of drunk driving accidents in court. The group sponsors bereavement workshops, community education speakers, and maintains an extensive library of drunk driving statistics and relevant information.

FURTHER INFORMATION/RESOURCES

MADD publishes *MADD in Action*, a quarterly newsletter; a periodic *MADD National Newsletter*; and the *MADDvocate*, twice a year. MADD also publishes numerous pamphlets, videos, books, and monographs that are available at no cost.

N

———————— / ————————

NATIONAL ASSOCIATION FOR THE ADVANCEMENT OF COLORED PEOPLE–LEGAL DEFENSE FUND (NAACP-LDF)
4805 Mt. Hope Drive
Baltimore, MD 21215
(212) 481–4100

ORGANIZATIONAL HISTORY/DEVELOPMENT

Established in 1939, the National Association for the Advancement of Colored People–Legal Defense Fund (NAACP-LDF) is one of the most prominent and respected civil rights organizations in the country. Now long involved in the spectrum of criminal justice issues, the organization gained prominence when a member lawyer, Thurgood Marshall, successfully argued for the mandatory desegregation of public schools before the U.S. Supreme Court in the landmark case *Brown* v. *Board of Education of Topeka Kansas*, 347 U.S. 483 (1954). Marshall, after being nominated by President Johnson on June 13, 1967, went on to serve as a Justice on the Court himself. The Legal Defense and Education Fund is the litigating arm of the NAACP. The NAACP, itself founded in 1909, currently has over 400,000 members, over 1,800 local affiliates, and a staff of about 130.

MISSION STATEMENT/PURPOSE

"To achieve equal rights through the democratic process and eliminate racial discrimination and prejudice by removing racial discrimination in housing, employment, voting, schools, the courts, transportation, recreation, prisons and business enterprises."

KEY POLICY ACTIVITY/CONCERNS

The NAACP is active in the areas of hate crimes and freedom of speech, the desegregation of public schools (see "Busing Could End After Supreme Court Decision," *New York Times*, April 1, 1992, p. A1), and the application of the death penalty in disproportionate levels to young minority men. The NAACP Legal Defense Fund sponsors training and informational seminars, tutorials, a job referral service, and maintains a law library. The organization recently opposed the nomination of Clarence Thomas to the U.S. Supreme Court upon the retirement of long-time NAACP advocate Supreme Court Justice Thurgood Marshall.

FURTHER INFORMATION/RESOURCES

The NAACP publishes *Crisis*, a newsletter (ten times per year), and an *Annual Report*.

NATIONAL ASSOCIATION OF BLACKS IN CRIMINAL JUSTICE (NABCJ)
P.O. Box 66271
Washington, DC 20035–6271
(405) 425–2513

ORGANIZATIONAL HISTORY/DEVELOPMENT

Founded in 1974 as a private/nonprofit organization made up of professionals working in the criminal justice system, the National Association of Blacks in Criminal Justice (NABCJ) monitors the impact of criminal justice policies on minority populations. The NABCJ currently has about 1,500 members and an annual budget of $50,000.

MISSION STATEMENT/PURPOSE

"To examine and act upon the needs, concerns, and contributions of African-Americans and other minorities as they relate to the administration of equal justice. Founded as a vehicle by which criminal justice practitioners could initiate positive change from within, while increasing opportunities for the average citizen to better understand the nature and operation of our local, state, and federal criminal justice process."

KEY POLICY ACTIVITY/CONCERNS

The NABCJ conducts regional training conferences and workshops in conjunction with the American Correctional Association.* The group also compiles statistics on minority involvement in the criminal justice system and makes available data to interested groups. The NABCJ has taken no formal position on legislation.

FURTHER INFORMATION/RESOURCES

The NABCJ publishes the *Local Criminal Justice Issues Newsletter*, the *NABCJ Newsletter*, and the *NABCJ Minority Criminal Justice Directory*.

NATIONAL ASSOCIATION OF CRIMINAL DEFENSE LAWYERS (NACDL)
Keith R. Stroup, Executive Director
1110 Vermont Avenue, Suite 1150
Washington, DC 20005
(202) 872–8688

ORGANIZATIONAL HISTORY/DEVELOPMENT

Established in 1958 and formerly titled National Association of Defense Lawyers in Criminal Cases (1973), the National Association of Criminal Defense Lawyers (NACDL) was founded to promote the skills, professionalism, and integrity of the defense bar and to serve as an alternative to the then all-white bar. NACDL hired its first staff in the mid-1970s and moved from Texas to Washington, D.C., in 1981. NACDL created the position of Legislative Director in 1985 (following the 1984 Crime Bill enactment) and in 1990 created the position of Public Affairs Director to help advance its policy goals. NACDL is a private, nonprofit organization with some 27,000 members (7,000 national plus some 20,000 in local affiliates) and an annual budget of over $1 million. NACDL is currently attempting to found the Institute for Criminal Defense Advocacy at California Western School of Law in San Diego, California.

MISSION STATEMENT/PURPOSE

"To promote professionalism, integrity, and the enhancement of skills of the defense bar; to serve as an alternative to the (then all-white) American Bar Association. To promote study and research in the field of criminal defense law and the related arts; to disseminate by lecture, seminars, and publications the advancement of the knowledge of the law as it relates to the field of criminal defense practice."

KEY POLICY ACTIVITY/CONCERNS

NACDL is an active participant in the criminal justice policy arena, having offered "friend of the court" briefs in numerous cases as well as *voir dire* (jury selection) services. NACDL offered its support toward the establishment of the Racial Justice Act, the National Commission on Root Causes of Crime and Drugs, and has also provided prison-impact assessments on pending sentencing legislation. NACDL has been opposed to the death penalty, to the repeal of the exclusionary rule, the diminishing of habeas corpus strictures, and mandatory minimum sentences in federal sentencing guidelines. NACDL holds a seat in the House of Delegates of the American Bar Association, with many ABA members also being members of the NACDL.

FURTHER INFORMATION/RESOURCES

NACDL publishes *The Champion*, a national magazine devoted to criminal defense lawyering. The group also publishes the *Washington Digest*, a monthly newsletter that seeks to update members on relevant legislative activity.

NATIONAL ASSOCIATION OF CRIMINAL JUSTICE PLANNERS (NACJP)
1331 H Street, NW, Suite 401
Washington, DC 20005
(202) 347–0501

ORGANIZATIONAL HISTORY/DEVELOPMENT

Established in 1973 as the National Association of Urban Criminal Justice Planning Directors, the National Association of Criminal Justice Planners (NACJP) started out as an organization designed to represent local interests in the Law Enforcement Assistance Administration's (LEAA) programs of the early 1970s. Since the disbanding of LEAA, the NACJP has focused particularly on the development of a national statistical series on felony sentencing outcomes. NACJP seeks to improve the technical skills of criminal justice planners and to institutionalize criminal justice planning generally. The group promotes communication in the areas of criminal justice planning and program development, while conducting research and compiling statistics. The NACJP today views its purpose more broadly than it has in the past, placing greater emphasis on facilitating an understanding of the criminal justice system for local practitioners, particularly in the area of funding decisions and how the decisions affect operations systemwide. This private, nonprofit organization containing roughly 200 members has an annual budget of over $300,000. NACJP membership consists primarily of persons directly involved in criminal justice planning at the national, state, and local levels.

MISSION STATEMENT/PURPOSE

"To represent local interests in the LEAA program" (1973). (Present) "To provide information to federal, state, and local criminal justice decision-makers; to communicate developments in criminal justice planning and program development; to conduct research surveys, conferences, and educational activities that enhance the public's understanding of criminal justice and the forces that affect criminal justice operations; to provide informational assistance to all persons and organizations involved in the criminal justice system; and to support the continuing development and implementation of standards to improve criminal justice."

KEY POLICY ACTIVITY/CONCERNS

The NACJP views its task today as one of providing guidance to local criminal justice planners and to that end has published numerous reports on the following subjects: "Administrative Concerns in Developing Standards and Goals"; "Survey Analysis of Local Criminal Justice Planning"; "Locally Funded Criminal Justice Planning"; "Preliminary Statistical Findings on the Costs and Operations of Police Patrol Cars"; "Preliminary Statistical Findings on Local Corrections"; "Beyond Crime: Law Enforcement Operational and Cost Data"; "A Sentencing Postscript: Felony Probationers Under Supervision in the Community"; "The Scales of Justice: Sentencing Outcomes in 28 Felony Courts, 1985"; and "The Scales of Justice: Sentencing Outcomes in 39 Felony Courts, 1986."

FURTHER INFORMATION/RESOURCES

The NACJP publishes an annual directory, an annual summary of its research activity titled *Research Findings*, and a semimonthly newsletter titled *News Update*.

NATIONAL ASSOCIATION OF DEFENSE LAWYERS IN CRIMINAL CASES

See National Association of Criminal Defense Lawyers.

NATIONAL ASSOCIATION OF JUVENILE CORRECTIONAL AGENCIES (NAJCA)

55 Albin Road
Bow, NH 03304–3703
(603) 271–5945

ORGANIZATIONAL HISTORY/DEVELOPMENT

Founded in 1903, the National Association of Juvenile Correctional Agencies (NAJCA) has gone through a long, involved process of historical evolution toward its current organizational form. Formerly titled the National Association of Training Schools and Juvenile Agencies (which was formed by an earlier merger between the National Association of Training Schools and the National Conference of Juvenile Agencies), the NAJCA presently consists of administrative and staff personnel of juvenile corrections residential facilities and other institutions charged with the care, training, and treatment of juveniles. In recent years, the NAJCA has attempted to broaden its focus on juvenile issues at the institutional level to include a more systemwide picture of juvenile issues, including child poverty and health care. In 1983, the NAJCA absorbed the Association of State Juvenile Justice Administrators (founded in 1968 and formerly titled the National Association of State Juvenile Delinquency Program Administrators). Today the NAJCA has about 400 members and an annual budget of $10,000.

MISSION STATEMENT/PURPOSE

"To disseminate ideas on the function, philosophy, and goals of the juvenile correctional field with emphasis on institutional rehabilitative programs. To promote evaluative research and foster progressive legislation; to encourage recruitment and retention of qualified personnel."

KEY POLICY ACTIVITY/CONCERNS

The NAJCA facilitates interaction between juvenile justice professionals, particularly those affiliated with institutions for juvenile care and treatment. The NAJCA cooperates with numerous juvenile agencies, providing information and technical assistance, promoting evaluative research, and encouraging enhanced training of juvenile justice practitioners. The NAJCA has actively promoted progressive modifications to the use and operation of juvenile institutions, particularly stressing rehabilitative programming and treatment. NAJCA cosponsors the American Correctional Congress and holds annual meetings.

FURTHER INFORMATION/RESOURCES

The NAJCA publishes its *Proceedings* annually, the *Newsletter NAJCA News* quarterly, and contributes to the publication of the *Journal for Juvenile Justice and Detention Services*.

NATIONAL ASSOCIATION OF LEGAL INVESTIGATORS (NALI)
c/o Lewis B. Knecht
Collins, Stecco & Wascha
717 S. Grand Traverse
Flint, MI 48502
(313) 767–5550

ORGANIZATIONAL HISTORY/DEVELOPMENT

Founded in 1937, the National Association of Legal Investigators (NALI) is a private, nonprofit organization whose membership consists of professional investigators in law firms and independent investigation companies who specialize in personal injury cases (both for the plaintiff and the defendant). The NALI seeks to "professionalize" the occupation of investigator through a series of certification programs, training seminars, and annual conferences. The NALI established its first certification program in 1973.

MISSION STATEMENT/PURPOSE

"To professionalize the legal investigator via seminars and professional certification programs."

KEY POLICY ACTIVITY/CONCERNS

The NALI has actively opposed efforts to establish "no-fault" insurance in the state of Michigan by engaging in direct mailing and political action committee support.

FURTHER INFORMATION/RESOURCES

The NALI publishes a bimonthly magazine, *Legal Investigator*, and holds an annual conference.

NATIONAL ASSOCIATION OF MUNICIPAL JUDGES
See American Judges Association.

NATIONAL ASSOCIATION OF STATE JUVENILE PROGRAM ADMINISTRATORS
See National Association of Juvenile Correctional Agencies.

NATIONAL ASSOCIATION OF TOWN WATCH (NATW)
P.O. Box 303
Seven Wynnewood Road, Suite 215
Wynnewood, PA 19096
(215) 649–7055
(800) NITE–OUT

ORGANIZATIONAL HISTORY/DEVELOPMENT

Established in 1981 as a private, nonprofit organization, the National Association of Town Watch (NATW) was founded to "heighten crime and drug prevention awareness; to generate support for local anti-crime efforts; to strengthen police/community relations; and to send a message to criminals letting them know that neighborhoods are organized and are fighting back." The NATW is responsible for organizing the annual "National Night Out" program, which seeks to promote community crime prevention and to assist the police in apprehending criminals. In 1988 President George Bush assisted in the launching of the National Night Out event. Today the NATW has a full-time staff of six and over 2,000 members, which are divided into local, state, and regional districts.

MISSION STATEMENT/PURPOSE

"To develop a network of exchange and information for organizations and agencies involved in police-affiliated crime watch programs. To promote, assist and encourage participation in community crime prevention by providing crime prevention groups with the opportunity to pool their resources, develop liaisons, and to share crime prevention tips and information on programs in their areas. To strengthen police/community camaraderie."

KEY POLICY ACTIVITY/CONCERNS

Calling itself the "nation's most powerful crime and drug prevention network," the NATW organizes and runs the nationwide "National Night Out" event in which community members across the United States and Canada spend time outside their homes one evening per year, usually in August, in symbolic support of neighborhood crime prevention efforts. Operating in some 8,000 communities across the United States and Canada, the National Night Out program is designed to strengthen police-community relations and to foster crime awareness. In addition, the NATW sponsors the "McGruff—Take a Bite Out of Crime" program, which seeks to enhance the awareness of children to crime, running programs in schools and other organizations like the YMCA. The NATW bestows its annual "Crimewatch" award to the city with the best "National Night Out" program.

FURTHER INFORMATION/RESOURCES

The National Association of Town Watch maintains a toll-free number: (800) NITE–OUT and publishes *New Spirit*, its quarterly newsletter. NATW also holds an annual convention.

NATIONAL ASSOCIATION OF TRAINING SCHOOLS AND JUVENILE AGENCIES
See National Association of Juvenile Correctional Agencies.

NATIONAL ASSOCIATION OF URBAN CRIMINAL JUSTICE PLANNING ADMINISTRATORS
See National Association of Criminal Justice Planners.

NATIONAL CATHOLIC WELFARE CONFERENCE
See U.S. Catholic Conference.

NATIONAL CATHOLIC WELFARE COUNCIL
See U.S. Catholic Conference.

NATIONAL CENTER FOR JUVENILE JUSTICE (NCJJ)
701 Forbes Avenue
Pittsburgh, PA 15219
(412) 227–6950

ORGANIZATIONAL HISTORY/DEVELOPMENT

Founded in 1973 as the research division of the National Council of Juvenile and Family Court Judges,[*] the National Center for Juvenile Justice (NCJJ) collects national statistics on juvenile court dispositions. In addition, the NCJJ conducts research evaluations and does its own independent research in the area of juvenile justice, usually by sponsoring visiting scholars.

MISSION STATEMENT/PURPOSE

None provided.

KEY POLICY ACTIVITY/CONCERNS

The NCJJ issues periodic statements on the state of juvenile justice in the United States and conducts its own research on various aspects of the juvenile justice system. Recently the group worked to establish the Office of Youth Services as a separate entity from the larger department of corrections, arguing that the department of corrections had too much to handle with its adults alone. The task of this new Office of Youth Services would be to develop programming for youths coming into contact with the court system and is currently being reviewed by a NCJJ task force.

FURTHER INFORMATION/RESOURCES

NCJJ publishes an annual collection of statistics, *Juvenile Court Statistics* and *KINDEX: An Index to Periodical Literature Concerning Children*, which chronicles legal periodicals that are devoted to juvenile justice issues. In addition, the NCJJ publishes numerous pamphlets, research reports, and position papers on relevant legislation.

NATIONAL CENTER FOR STATE COURTS (NCSC)
Larry L. Sipes, President
300 Newport Avenue
Williamsburg, VA 23187
(804) 253–2000

ORGANIZATIONAL HISTORY/DEVELOPMENT

Established in 1971 as a private, nonprofit organization designed to assist in the administration of justice in the country's state courts, the National Center for State Courts (NCSC) provides assistance to state and local trial and appellate courts to improve their administration of justice. The NCSC particularly concentrates its services in the areas of research, technical, and clerical services. In addition, NCSC furnishes consultant services to the state courts and conducts national studies and projects for the enhancement of state court operation. The organization acts as a clearinghouse for exchange of information on court problems and coordinates interorganizational involvement, particularly at the judicial level. With an annual budget of $12.2 million and a staff of 130, NCSC is composed of fifty representatives from U.S. state courts and five representatives from the U.S. courts in American territories.

MISSION STATEMENT/PURPOSE

"To help the state courts improve their ability to administer justice."

KEY POLICY ACTIVITY/CONCERNS

The NCSC is one of the most active national-level organizations in the area of the courts, being directly involved, to varying degrees, in the administration of every state and territorial court in the country. The NCSC conducts research and compiles statistics on the case loads of all the state and territorial courts in addition to conducting research on a range of topics from community dispute resolution to alternatives to incarceration and jury management. In 1990 the NCSC conducted more than sixty direct assistance programs to state courts and has become a vital part of the American judicial system at the state court level.

FURTHER INFORMATION/RESOURCES

The National Center for State Courts publishes an *Annual Report*, *Judicial Salary Review* (semiannually), *Report* (monthly), and *State Court Journal* (a monthly newsletter). NCSC holds an annual board meeting.

References

Flango, Victor E., Robert T. Roper, and Mary E. Elsner. (1983). *The Business of State Trial Courts*. Williamsburg, VA: National Center for State Courts.

Miller, J.L., Marilyn Roberts, and Charlotte A. Carter. (1981). *Sentencing Reform: A Review and Annotated Bibliography*. Williamsburg, VA: National Center for State Courts.

National Conference on the Judiciary. (1978). *State Courts, a Blueprint for the Future: Proceedings of the Second National Conference on the Judiciary*. Williamsburg, VA: National Center for State Courts.

NATIONAL CENTER FOR YOUTH LAW–YOUTH LAW CENTER (NCYL)

Mark I. Soler, Executive Director
114 Sansome Street, Suite 900
San Francisco, CA 94104
(415) 543–3307

ORGANIZATIONAL HISTORY/DEVELOPMENT

Founded in 1978 as a private, nonprofit organization devoted to addressing the needs of juveniles lacking resources to obtain legal council when necessary, the National Center for Youth Law (NCYL) currently employs six full-time attorneys devoted to protecting the rights and well-being of juveniles across the country. The NCYL currently has an annual budget of over $1 million.

MISSION STATEMENT/PURPOSE

"The mission of the Youth Law Center is to preserve and protect the rights, health, and lives of children at risk. Youth Law Center programs focus on the problems of low-income and underserved children, especially those who are incarcerated or placed outside their families. The Center's hope is to intervene on behalf of children and youth at critical junctures in their lives to improve treatment and conditions to which they are subject, and thereby positively affect their futures. The work of the Youth Law Center addresses the problems of individuals with the intent of bringing about changes for large numbers of children. Toward these ends, the Youth Law Center's goals are to: A) Effect positive change in conditions and treatment of poor children in various forms of custody; B) Advocate for legislative and other reforms affecting the legal rights of children and youth; C) Provide specialized information, advice, and other support in youth law matters to parents and children in need, public officials, legal services organizations, private attorneys, health care professionals, social workers, and others working on behalf of children; D) Disseminate information on the legal rights of children.''

KEY POLICY ACTIVITY/CONCERNS

Some examples of work done recently by the NCYL include the center's monitoring of placement procedures for children in new orphanages; the provision of in-court training for law practitioners involved in youth/child law cases; assisting in the development of improved youth law standards on numerous Native-American Indian reservations in conjunction with tribal councils and leadership; staff attorneys published an article in a prominent law review on the issues of integrating child and family legal services.

FURTHER INFORMATION/RESOURCES

The NCYL publishes the *Youth Law News*, bimonthly, and an *Annual Report*.

NATIONAL CENTER ON INSTITUTIONS AND ALTERNATIVES (NCIA)
Jerome Miller, President
635 Slaters Lane, Suite G–100
Alexandria, VA 22314
(703) 684–0373

ORGANIZATIONAL HISTORY/DEVELOPMENT

Established in 1977 as a private, nonprofit organization devoted to the promotion of alternatives to incarceration, the National Center on Institutions and Alternatives (NCIA) serves primarily as a clearinghouse for information regarding alternatives to prison. Currently the NCIA has a full-time staff of fifty and an annual budget of over $1.5 million.

MISSION STATEMENT/PURPOSE

''To promote the study and implementation of alternatives to the use of prisons and mental hospitals.''

KEY POLICY ACTIVITY/CONCERNS

The primary activity of the NCIA has been the collection and dissemination of information regarding the state of corrections and alternatives to prisons and mental hospitals to interested organizations throughout the country. In terms of criminal justice policy, the NCIA has been particularly interested in the issues of jail/prison suicide, the death penalty, and child abuse. The NCIA promotes the utilization of its Client Specific Planning Program, a rigid, structured alternative sentencing scheme to be used by the courts when those convicted are mentally ill. The NCIA promotes group therapy services and offers crisis intervention assistance for the mentally ill. Most recently, the organization came out against the imposition of mandatory life sentences with no parole for sex offenders.

In addition to these activities, the NCIA has actively promoted the use of artistic expression as a therapeutic device for the mentally ill and incarcerated. Along these lines, the NCIA sponsors the Augustus Institute, a mental health center for juveniles and adults in addition to its Firebird Gallery, an art gallery that displays and encourages the exhibition of works by institutionalized persons. The group holds an annual conference.

FURTHER INFORMATION/RESOURCES

The NCIA publishes *Augustus: A Journal of Progressive Human Services* monthly; the influential *Scared Straight: A Second Look* (pamphlet); *Juvenile Decarceration: The Politics of Correctional Reform*, a book-length manuscript; and *Darkness Closes In: National Study of Jail Suicides*, a monograph.

References

Feeley, Malcolm. (1983). *Executive Summary Report on Client Specific Planning: A Project of the National Center on Institutions and Alternatives*. New Haven, CT: Silbert, Feeley and Associates, Inc.
————. (1983). *Report on Client Specific Planning: A Project of the National Center on Institutions and Alternatives*. New Haven, CT: Silbert, Feeley and Associates, Inc.

NATIONAL CHIEFS OF POLICE UNION
See International Association of Chiefs of Police.

NATIONAL CITIZEN'S COMMITTEE FOR THE RIGHT TO KEEP AND BEAR ARMS
See Citizen's Committee for the Right to Keep and Bear Arms.

NATIONAL COALITION AGAINST DOMESTIC VIOLENCE (NCADV)
P.O. Box 34103
Washington, DC 20043–4103
(202) 638–6388

ORGANIZATIONAL HISTORY/DEVELOPMENT

Founded in 1978 as a private, nonprofit organization devoted to assisting female victims of domestic violence, the National Coalition Against Domestic Violence (NCADV) has fifty member groups across the country and helps in the maintenance of over 1,200 battered women's shelters.

MISSION STATEMENT/PURPOSE

Not available.

KEY POLICY ACTIVITY/CONCERNS

NCADV is actually a coalition of numerous grassroots level battered women's shelters and resource agencies across the country. NCADV seeks to facilitate training of personnel, provide technical assistance to developing shelters, and make referrals in cooperation with other agencies. One important theme for NCADV has been the alarming degree to which women with children have found themselves economically dependent on outside funding sources while raising their children. NCADV has actively sought to remove barriers hindering mothers from entering the workplace and has assisted women in establishing economic independence. NCADV currently has over 1,200 local groups/shelters and puts out numerous publications and informational pamphlets.

FURTHER INFORMATION/RESOURCES

NCADV publishes the *National Coalition Against Domestic Violence—Voice* quarterly and *A Step Toward Independence: Toward Economic Self-Sufficiency*.

NATIONAL COALITION AGAINST SEXUAL ASSAULT (NCASA)
Marybeth Carter, President
P.O. Box 21378
Washington, DC 20009
(202) 483–7165

ORGANIZATIONAL HISTORY/DEVELOPMENT

Founded in 1978, the National Coalition Against Sexual Assault (NCASA), is a private, nonprofit organization devoted to public education about sexual assault, particularly sexual assault against women. NCASA is one of the most well-respected victim-advocate groups assisting female rape victims in the United States. NCASA currently has over 500 members.

MISSION STATEMENT/PURPOSE

Not available.

KEY POLICY ACTIVITY/CONCERNS

NCASA sponsors public education programs on issues of sexual assault against women and actively assists female victims of rape by acting as a resource/ counseling agency. NCASA has been particularly effective in establishing a network of individuals and resource contacts who assist women rape victims and stress victim survival tactics. NCASA also disseminates statistical information on sexual assault via its public education programs and encourages awareness of this widespread, often unreported problem.

FURTHER INFORMATION/RESOURCES

NCASA publishes a quarterly newsletter.

NATIONAL COLLEGE OF DISTRICT ATTORNEYS (NCDA)
University of Houston
Law Center
Houston, TX 77204–6380
(713) 747–6232

ORGANIZATIONAL HISTORY/DEVELOPMENT

Founded in 1969, the National College of District Attorneys (NCDA) is a private, nonprofit organization made up of federal, state, and local prosecutors, military lawyers, and assistant attorneys general. In 1970 NCDA established and offered its first Career Prosecutor Course; in 1972, its regional continuing education programs began; and in 1973 NCDA developed its executive prosecutor program. NCDA is sponsored by the American Bar Association* and the National District Attorneys Association.* In 1991 NCDA was declared to be the training arm of the National District Attorneys Association. Today the NCDA has a full-time staff of fifteen and an annual budget of over $1.5 million.

MISSION STATEMENT/PURPOSE

"To provide high-quality post-graduate legal education and training for lawyers engaged in public prosecution; to increase the knowledge and skills of the prosecutor; to develop the professionalism and confidence of the prosecutor in coping with the challenges and opportunities of the office; and to afford the opportunity for exchange of information and ideas among prosecutors."

KEY POLICY ACTIVITY/CONCERNS

The NCDA engages in the training and continuing education of local, state, and federal prosecutors and assistant attorneys general. The NCDA has taken no formal positions on legislation and engages in no lobbying, direct mailing, or other political activity.

FURTHER INFORMATION/RESOURCES

The NCDA publishes a newsletter, *Oyez* (ten times per year), and the *Bibliographic Guide for Prosecutors* (annually).

NATIONAL COMMITTEE AGAINST REPRESSIVE LEGISLATION (NCARL)

Ruth Calvin-Anderson, Cochair
1313 W. 8th Street, Suite 313
Los Angeles, CA 90017
(213) 484–6661

ORGANIZATIONAL HISTORY/DEVELOPMENT

Founded in 1960 as a private, nonprofit organization, the National Committee Against Repressive Legislation (NCARL) was formerly known as the National Committee to Abolish the House Un-American Activities Committee (HUAC) (1969), and the National Committee to Abolish HUAC/HISC (1970). The organization was founded by Frank Wilkinson, who later became the first person sent to prison for not answering questions about his personal associations and friendships during the so-called "Red Scare" in testimony before the House Un-American Activities Committee. Wilkinson's case went all the way to the Supreme Court and in a landmark 5–4 decision the high Court upheld his conviction for "contempt of Congress." In 1987 it was revealed that the Federal Bureau of Investigation had been secretly surveilling Wilkinson since 1942 when he had been an activist for the homeless in the Watts area of Los Angeles. The FBI had accused Wilkinson of being a Communist.

Since the abolition of the House Un-American Activities Committee in 1975 (with the implementation of the Federal Privacy Act), NCARL has continued to focus its attention on what the group considers to be "political spying" by FBI and other federal law enforcement and national security agencies.

MISSION STATEMENT/PURPOSE

"To abolish the House Committee on Un-American Activities (HUAC)."

KEY POLICY ACTIVITY/CONCERNS

The NCARL engages in lobbying, direct mailing, political action committee activity, and grassroots organizing at the local level. NCARL's primary dedication is to the protection of the First Amendment. Recently, NCARL has been successful in gleaning documents from the Federal Bureau of Investigation regarding its "COINTELPRO" (counterintelligence program) operations in which that agency covertly surveilled many private citizens and organizations. In addition, the group worked in coalition with the Japanese American Citizens League to repeal Title II of the International Security Act of 1950, the "Detention Centers Act," and is currently trying to initiate a ban on covert operations by the CIA.

FURTHER INFORMATION/RESOURCES

NCARL publishes the *FBI Petition News*, a periodical; *Right to Know*, and *Freedom to Act*.

NATIONAL COMMITTEE TO ABOLISH THE HOUSE UN-AMERICAN ACTIVITIES COMMITTEE

See National Committee Against Repressive Legislation.

NATIONAL CONFERENCE OF JUVENILE AGENCIES

See National Association of Juvenile Correctional Agencies.

NATIONAL CONFERENCE OF STATE CRIMINAL JUSTICE PLANNING ADMINISTRATORS

See National Criminal Justice Association.

NATIONAL CONFERENCE OF STATE LEGISLATIVE LEADERS

See National Conference of State Legislators.

NATIONAL CONFERENCE OF STATE LEGISLATORS (NCSL)

William T. Pound, Executive Director
1050 17th Street, Suite 2100
Denver, CO 80265
(303) 623–7800

ORGANIZATIONAL HISTORY/DEVELOPMENT

Founded in 1975 as a private, nonprofit organization composed of national state legislators and their staffs, the National Conference of State Legislators (NCSL) coordinates information on various state policy positions for use at the federal and state levels. The NCSL was formed by a merger of the National Legislative Conference, the National Conference of State Legislative Leaders, and the National Society of State Legislators. The NCSL currently has a staff of 140 and an annual budget of about $8 million.

MISSION STATEMENT/PURPOSE

"To improve the quality and effectiveness of state legislators; to ensure states a strong, cohesive voice in the federal decision-making process; to foster interstate communication and cooperation."

KEY POLICY ACTIVITY/CONCERNS

The NCSL maintains the Office of State-Federal Relations in Washington, D.C., and seeks to improve communication among state governments for the enhancement of public policy at both the state and federal levels. The organization assembles research data and disseminates it, maintains an extensive library, conducts workshops and seminars on various legislative initiatives, and provides technical assistance.

FURTHER INFORMATION/RESOURCES

The NCSL publishes its bimonthly *Federal Update*, its bimonthly *Fiscal Letter*, and the *State Legislatures* magazine ten times per year. The organization also publishes "handbooks" for state legislators on various issues.

NATIONAL COUNCIL OF JUVENILE AND FAMILY COURT JUDGES (NCJFCJ)

Louis W. McHardy, Executive Director
University of Nevada
P.O. Box 8970
Reno, NV 89557
(702) 784–6012

ORGANIZATIONAL HISTORY/DEVELOPMENT

Founded in 1937 as a private, nonprofit organization devoted to promoting the concept of a "noncriminal" tribunal for juveniles, the National Council of Juvenile and Family Court Judges (NCJFCJ) is composed of judges who have juvenile or family court jurisdictions and of others interested in the adjudication of juvenile and family matters. The NCJFCJ was formerly titled the National Council of Juvenile Court Judges (1977). The NCJFCJ currently has over 2,500 members, a full-time staff of fifty, and an annual budget of about $5 million. In 1969, NCJFCJ left the American Bar Center in Chicago to relocate on the campus of University of Nevada, Reno.

MISSION STATEMENT/PURPOSE

"To improve the standards, practices, and effectiveness of the juvenile courts and other courts exercising jurisdiction over families and children. To inform or assist persons or agencies with jurisdiction over families and children; to educate persons serving in or otherwise connected to the juvenile court. To further more effective administration of justice for young people through the improvement of juvenile and family court standards and practices. To promote the concept of a 'non-criminal' tribunal for juveniles; and to promote the concept of treatment for disturbed youth and protection for the abused and neglected juvenile."

KEY POLICY ACTIVITY/CONCERNS

Addressing itself primarily to the state and federal levels of policy formation, the NCJFCJ compiles and disseminates research data for judges and other court personnel, primarily on juvenile and family law issues. The organization sponsors the Permanency Planning Project, which monitors the status of juveniles in the nations' court systems. In 1990, the organization actively supported Public Law 96–272, which promoted the reauthorization of the Office of Juvenile Justice and Delinquency Prevention (OJJDP) housed in the Department of Justice. In addition to these activities, the NCJFCJ sponsors continuing education classes for juvenile court judges and court personnel, offers technical (statistical) assistance to these courts, and publishes numerous pamphlets, monographs, and books.

FURTHER INFORMATION/RESOURCES

The NCJFCJ publishes the *Juvenile and Family Court Journal*, which comes out quarterly; the *Juvenile and Family Law Digest*, a monthly case-law digest; the *Journal and Family Court Newsletter*, bimonthly; and the *National Council on Juvenile and Family Court Judges–Directory*, which comes out annually.

NATIONAL COUNCIL OF JUVENILE COURT JUDGES
See National Council of Juvenile and Family Court Judges.

NATIONAL COUNCIL ON CHILD ABUSE AND FAMILY VIOLENCE (NCCAFV)
Alan Davis, Director
1155 Connecticut Avenue, NW, Suite 300
Washington, DC 20036
(202) 429–6695

ORGANIZATIONAL HISTORY/DEVELOPMENT

Founded in 1984 as a private, nonprofit organization devoted to providing assistance to women and children victims of domestic violence, the National Council on Child Abuse and Family Violence (NCCAFV) works to disseminate information on like organizations throughout the country and gathers statistics on domestic violence.

MISSION STATEMENT/PURPOSE

Not available.

KEY POLICY ACTIVITY/CONCERNS

The NCCAFV assists in the development of training programs for volunteer workers in domestic violence shelters, provides technical assistance to developing shelters around the country, and stresses the cyclical nature of domestic violence. Of particular importance to NCCAFV has been the so-called intergenerational "cycle" of violence often present in families, in that victims of abuse in the home are often unable to be nonabusive themselves later in life. NCCAFV has therefore been an active sponsor of community-based alternatives for domestic violence offenders and has provided assistance to victims of domestic violence.

FURTHER INFORMATION/RESOURCES

NCCAFV publishes a newsletter periodically titled *INFORUM*. The organization also publishes numerous informational pamphlets on domestic violence, child and elder abuse.

NATIONAL COUNCIL ON CRIME AND DELINQUENCY (NCCD)
Barry A. Krisberg, President
685 Market Street, Suite 620
San Francisco, CA 94105
(415) 896–6223

ORGANIZATIONAL HISTORY/DEVELOPMENT

Established in 1907 as a private, nonprofit organization designed to support probation and court services for juveniles and adults in the criminal justice system, the National Council on Crime and Delinquency (NCCD) was formerly titled the American Parole Association and the National Probation Association. During the period from the 1920s through the 1950s, the organization was responsible for developing guidelines to be used in numerous state juvenile court systems. The NCCD is currently made up of criminal justice professionals interested in the issues of juvenile delinquency, community-based programs, corrections, and crime prevention.

MISSION STATEMENT/PURPOSE

"To support probation and court services for juveniles and adults in the criminal justice system."

KEY POLICY ACTIVITY/CONCERNS

The NCCD provides technical assistance to state governments in the areas of criminal justice research and policy development. Specifically, the NCCD offers projections of offender and inmate populations in concert with pending legislation, participates in juvenile justice and child welfare case management, and has actively opposed the lowering of age of adult court jurisdiction in juvenile cases. The NCCD supported California's Youth Authority Sentencing Program, which sought to reduce both the size and the level of overcrowding in California's institutions for juveniles. The council is well known for having developed its Model Sentencing Act in 1957, versions of which were adopted by many states.

The council is active in criminal justice research and policy development, especially in the areas of juvenile justice and child welfare case management.

The council also assists in the development and implementation of model criminal justice programs in a variety of areas for state and local governments. The NCCD was formerly known as the National Probation and Parole Association (1960).

FURTHER INFORMATION/RESOURCES

The NCCD publishes two journals, *Crime and Delinquency* and the *Journal of Research in Crime and Delinquency*.

NATIONAL COUNCIL TO CONTROL HANDGUNS
See Handgun Control, Inc.

NATIONAL CRIME PREVENTION COUNCIL (NCPC)
John A. Calhoon, Executive Director
1700 K Street, NW, Second Floor
Washington, DC 20006
(202) 466–6272

ORGANIZATIONAL HISTORY/DEVELOPMENT

Established in 1982 as a private, nonprofit organization devoted to crime prevention, the National Crime Prevention Council (NCPC) is a nonmembership organization that cosponsors the well-known "McGruff the Crime Dog" program with the National Association of Town Watch*, sponsors public service announcements, and the "Take a Bite Out of Crime" programs in public schools and communities. The NCPC has organized the "Crime Prevention Coalition," a confederation of over 120 citizens groups, businesses, and law enforcement agencies that assist in sponsoring NCPC's many community block programs, "neighborhood watch" efforts, and community service programs. The NCPC currently has a staff of thirty-eight and an annual budget of over $5 million.

MISSION STATEMENT/PURPOSE

The NCPC generally seeks to "expand the concept of crime prevention beyond individual self-protection to encompass proactive efforts at neighborhood revitalization and other aspects of positive social change; . . . to forge a nationwide commitment by people acting individually and together to prevent crime and build safer and more caring communities; to convince citizens and policy makers to give top priority to prevention, rather than after-the-fact strategies."

KEY POLICY ACTIVITY/CONCERNS

From 1986 through 1989, the NCPC sponsored the Indiana "Youth As Resources" project, which established grant-making authority to local adults and youth and sought to integrate the community into active decision-making bodies. More than 4,000 youth took part in over 200 projects, which consisted primarily of neighborhood clean-up efforts and crime prevention education. The NCPC sponsors the "Take a Bite Out of Crime" programs in schools and communities, with "McGruff the Crime Dog" as its mascot. The NCPC also helped establish numerous "Neighborhood Watch" programs in many U.S. communities. Lastly, the NCPC provides training and technical assistance to youth groups, law enforcement, and the public schools and bestows crime prevention awards annually. The NCPC has taken no formal positions on criminal justice legislation or policy and is primarily concerned with activity at the city and county levels.

FURTHER INFORMATION/RESOURCES

The NCPC publishes numerous books, posters, pamphlets, newsletters, and other material. Some titles include *Challenges and Opportunities in Drug Prevention: A Demand Reduction Resource Guide for Law Enforcement Officers*; *Ink & Airtime: Working Effectively with the Media*; *Violence, Youth, and a Way Out* (pamphlet); *Preventing Crime in Urban Communities: Handbook and Program Profiles*. A newsletter, *Catalyst*, is also published ten times per year.

NATIONAL CRIMINAL JUSTICE ASSOCIATION (NCJA)
444 N. Capitol Street, NW, Suite 608
Washington, DC 20001
(202) 347-4900

ORGANIZATIONAL HISTORY/DEVELOPMENT

Established in 1971 as a private, nonprofit organization, the National Criminal Justice Association (NCJA) is made up of state and local criminal justice planners, prosecutors, police chiefs, elected officials, and researchers. Initially devoted to representing the interests of state executives charged with the administration of the former Law Enforcement Assistance Administration program, the NCJA today works closely with the National Governor's Association* and the National Conference of State Legislators.*

The primary task of the NCJA today is to represent the states in public policy matters related to crime control and to assist in the unification and dissemination of state views on criminal justice issues before Congress. Having evolved from an organization whose existence was centered around a U.S. Department of Justice federal aid program, the NCJA now represents a broad range of justice-related interests and has considerable autonomy via grants and contract work. The organization has recently focused its attention on national criminal justice policy, with a particular emphasis on the "drug war." The organization's current membership is about 1,200, and it has an annual budget of $800,000. The NCJA was formerly titled the National Conference of State Criminal Justice Planning Administrators (1980).

MISSION STATEMENT/PURPOSE

"To provide a formal mechanism for developing unified state views on topical criminal justice issues and for informing Congress, the governors, and other national, state, and local public and private interests of the states' public safety needs and accomplishments."

KEY POLICY ACTIVITY/CONCERNS

The NCJA seeks to influence national-level policy formation through the dissemination of state views of particular criminal and juvenile justice issues, pending legislation, and criminal justice planning. While NCJA does not generally oppose or support a particular bill, the organization is an active participant in the drafting of the language used in many pieces of criminal justice legislation. That is to say that the NCJA is not an "issue-specific" group in any sense, but is very active in the formation of criminal justice policy generally via its role as a representative of the states before Congress. The organization functions by working closely with the National Governors' Association and the National Conference of State Legislators, among other state and local groups. The NCJA also holds an annual conference, conducts training seminars, and provides technical assistance to state agencies in the areas of criminal and juvenile justice planning.

FURTHER INFORMATION/RESOURCES

The NCJA publishes the following titles: *A Summary Review of Issues and Pending Legislation at the Federal Level in Subject Areas Covered by the NGA/ NCJA Survey on States' Organized Crime and Drug Trafficking Laws and Related Enforcement Tools*, May 1984; the *Justice Bulletin*, a monthly NCJA newsletter; *Justice Research*, a bimonthly newsletter; and *Juvenile Justice*, a newsletter devoted to covering federal and state legislative proposals in the area of juvenile justice.

NATIONAL DISTRICT ATTORNEYS ASSOCIATION (NDAA)
Jack Yelverton, Executive Director
1033 N. Fairfax Street, Suite 200
Alexandria, VA 22314
(703) 549–9222

ORGANIZATIONAL HISTORY/DEVELOPMENT

Founded in 1950 as a private, nonprofit organization the National District Attorneys Association (NDAA) is devoted to assisting prosecutors, assistant prosecutors, paralegals, and other prosecutorial staff. The NDAA currently has over 7,000 members and a staff of twenty.

MISSION STATEMENT/PURPOSE

None provided.

KEY POLICY ACTIVITY/CONCERNS

The NDAA acts as an information clearinghouse, providing judges and prosecutors with information on landmark cases, research findings, and other technical assistance. The NDAA is also active in the area of the courts, having recently established its National Traffic Law Center for judges and prosecutors in Washington, D.C., for example. In addition, the NDAA operates the National Center for the Prosecution of Child Abuse in Arlington, Virginia. The organization releases statements and policy position papers on criminal justice issues and is active in the prosecutorial arm of the criminal justice system. Most recently, the NDAA issued a statement condemning rap artist "ICE-T" for his release of a song titled "Cop Killer," in which the artist advocates the killing of police officers in response to perceived police brutality ("Ice-T Withdraws 'Cop Killer' Song; Embattled Rapper Cites Death Threats," *Washington Times*, July 29, 1992, p. A1). The group holds an annual national conference.

FURTHER INFORMATION/RESOURCES

NDAA publishes numerous informational pamphlets and monographs on relevant issues.

NATIONAL GOVERNOR'S ASSOCIATION (NGA)
Hall of States
444 N. Capitol Street NE
Washington, DC 20001
(202) 624–5300

ORGANIZATIONAL HISTORY/DEVELOPMENT

Founded in 1908 and formerly titled the Governor's Conference and then the National Governor's Conference, the National Governor's Association (NGA) is composed of the fifty state governors and the governors of Guam, American Samoa, the Virgin Islands, the Northern Mariana Islands, and Puerto Rico. The NGA's key operational task is to provide the branches of the federal government information on the needs and policy interests of the states and territories. The NGA has fifty-five members, a staff of one hundred, and an annual budget of $10 million.

MISSION STATEMENT/PURPOSE

None provided.

KEY POLICY ACTIVITY/CONCERNS

The NGA is a highly influential policy organization, taking positions on the full spectrum of national policy issues—including many in criminal justice. The NGA's Center for Policy Research conducts research and evaluations of various state programs across the country and utilizes these findings in its policy statements. Representatives of the NGA frequently testify before legislative committees at both the state and national levels.

FURTHER INFORMATION/RESOURCES

The NGA has a long list of publications, including *Federal Funds Information for States*, a periodic newsletter; the *Governor's Weekly Bulletin*; its semiannual *Policy Positions*; and its annual *President's Budget: Impact on the States*.

NATIONAL GOVERNOR'S CONFERENCE
See National Governor's Association.

NATIONAL JAIL ASSOCIATION
See American Jail Association.

NATIONAL JAIL MANAGERS ASSOCIATION
See American Jail Association.

NATIONAL JUVENILE RESTITUTION ASSOCIATION
See American Restitution Association.

NATIONAL LAWYERS GUILD (NLG)
Barbara Dudley, Executive Director
55 Avenue of the Americas
New York, NY 10013
(212) 966–5000

ORGANIZATIONAL HISTORY/DEVELOPMENT

The National Lawyers Guild (NLG) was founded in 1937 and is made up of lawyers, law students, legal professionals (e.g., paralegals), and so-called inmates interested in the law. The NLG currently has over 9,000 members and an annual budget of about $275,000.

MISSION STATEMENT/PURPOSE

"The National Lawyers Guild is an association dedicated to the need for basic change in the structure of our political and economic system. We seek to unite the lawyers, law students, legal workers, and jailhouse lawyers of America in an organization which shall function as an effective political and social force in the service of the people, to the end that human rights shall be regarded as more sacred than property interests. Our aim is to bring together all those who regard adjustments to new conditions as more important than the veneration of precedent; who recognize the importance of safeguarding and extending the rights of workers, women, farmers, and minority groups upon whom the welfare of the entire nation depends; who seek actively to eliminate racism; who work to maintain and protect our civil rights and liberties in the face of persistent attacks upon them; and who look upon the law as an instrument for the protection of the people, rather than for their repression."

KEY POLICY ACTIVITY/CONCERNS

The National Lawyers Guild refers to itself as a "progressive legal aid organization" and has consistently been involved in prisoners' rights issues, the protection of due process procedures, and the provision of legal services to indigent defendants. In addition, the organization maintains committees devoted to affirmative action, immigration, gay rights, and a number of other topics. The organization has been opposed to the use of inhumane treatment in prisons, particularly the use of solitary confinement—for both women and men—and the holding of political prisoners in U.S. prisons. The NGL has also been concerned about the increasingly widespread reduction in funding for court-appointed defense counsel.

FURTHER INFORMATION/RESOURCES

The NLG publishes the *National Lawyers Guild—Guild Notes*, bimonthly; the *National Lawyers Guild—Guild Practitioner*, quarterly; the *National Lawyers Guild—Referral Directory*, twice per year; and *On Watch*, a bimonthly newsletter. The NLG also publishes numerous position papers and books on topics ranging from civil liberties and nuclear disarmament to the rights of tenants.

NATIONAL LEGISLATIVE CONFERENCE
See National Conference of State Legislators.

NATIONAL ORGANIZATION FOR REFORM OF MARIJUANA LAWS (NORML)
1636 R Street, NW, Number 3
Washington, DC 20009
(202) 483–5500

ORGANIZATIONAL HISTORY/DEVELOPMENT

Founded in 1970 as a private, nonprofit organization devoted to the legalization of marijuana possession in the United States, the National Organization for Reform of Marijuana Laws (NORML) actively supports efforts to legalize personal use of marijuana for recreational and medicinal purposes. Since the federal banning of the use of marijuana in 1937, several efforts at "decriminalization" (the elimination of criminal penalties) for marijuana possession have occurred. "Th[is] movement toward decriminalization began in 1973 with Oregon, followed by Colorado, Alaska, Ohio, and California in 1975; Mississippi, North Carolina, and New York in 1977; and Nebraska in 1978" (James A. Inciardi, *The War on Drugs: Heroin, Cocaine, Crime and Public Policy* [Palo Alto, CA: Mayfield Publishing Co., 1986] p. 36). Since the 1970s, however, and particularly with the implementation of the Reagan administration's "zero tolerance for casual drug use" policies in the 1980s, possession of marijuana has been increasingly restricted and "recriminalized." In Alaska, for example, where possession of small amounts (up to four ounces) of marijuana was "legalized" in 1975, in 1990 marijuana possession was recriminalized. NORML has been an active participant in each of the "decriminalization" initiatives mentioned above. Today with over 7,000 members nationwide and an annual budget of close to $500,000, NORML is the most active "single-interest" group involved in this issue.

MISSION STATEMENT/PURPOSE

"To attain the legalization of marijuana possession, use and cultivation in the United States, as well as to reduce government regulation of commercial transactions; . . . to provide the government a more effective influence over marijuana use than the current policy of attempting to maintain a total prohibition on both the use and supply of marijuana."

KEY POLICY ACTIVITY/CONCERNS

The NORML supports the legalized use of marijuana for medicinal and recreational purposes and has actively supported efforts at "decriminalization" of marijuana possession. The group has opposed mandatory minimum sentencing schemes for marijuana possession and use, drug testing in all forms, and all recriminalization efforts. NORML is currently sponsoring a pending challenge to the recriminalization of marijuana possession in Alaska in the state Supreme Court.

FURTHER INFORMATION/RESOURCES

The NORML publishes a seasonal newspaper titled *The Leaflet*, as well as a seasonal newsletter, the *Citizen's Guide to Marijuana Laws*.

NATIONAL ORGANIZATION FOR VICTIM ASSISTANCE (NOVA)
1757 Park Road, NW
Washington, DC 20010
(202) 232–6682

ORGANIZATIONAL HISTORY/DEVELOPMENT

Founded in 1975 as a private, nonprofit organization devoted to addressing the concerns of victims of crimes in the criminal justice system, the National Organization for Victim Assistance (NOVA) currently has over 4,500 members and an annual budget of over $1 million. NOVA has a full-time staff of sixteen and is one of the major victim's rights groups in the country.

MISSION STATEMENT/PURPOSE

"To express forcefully the victim's claims, too long ignored, for decency, compassion, and justice; to press those claims for the victims of crime and also for the victims of other stark misfortunes; and to ensure that victims' rights are honored by government officials and all others who can aid in the victims' relief and recovery."

KEY POLICY ACTIVITY/CONCERNS

NOVA is composed of professionals working in the criminal justice system, and in related fields, who work to assist victims of crime. NOVA offers technical assistance to developing victims' assistance programs and to programs designed to train volunteer counselors who will deal with victims of crime. NOVA sponsors its Victim Assistance Training Program and its National Victims' Rights Week. One of the strengths of NOVA is that it has established a national network of victims' assistance professionals and can assist groups at the local level by making referrals to various regional offices or contact persons. One of NOVA's primary tasks is working as a clearinghouse on victims' assistance information.

FURTHER INFORMATION/RESOURCES

NOVA publishes the *National Organization for Victim Assistance—Newsletter*, monthly, and its annual directory of victim assistance programs *Victim Assistance Programs and Resources*.

NATIONAL PRISON ASSOCIATION
See American Correctional Association.

NATIONAL PRISON PROJECT OF THE ACLU (NPP)
1875 Connecticut Avenue, NW, Suite 410
Washington, DC 20009
(202) 234–4830

ORGANIZATIONAL HISTORY/DEVELOPMENT

Founded in 1972 in the wake of the Attica Prison riot, this private, nonprofit organization is a project of the American Civil Liberties Union (ACLU) and seeks to protect the constitutional rights of prisoners and to improve prison conditions via litigation and public education. The NPP has a full-time staff of twenty and an annual budget of over $1.5 million.

MISSION STATEMENT/PURPOSE

"To strengthen and protect prisoners' Eighth Amendment (protection from cruel and unusual punishments) and other Constitutional rights through litigation and other channels."

KEY POLICY ACTIVITY/CONCERNS

The NPP's principal activity is litigation. The organization has won sweeping statewide reforms regarding the conditions of prisons in Alabama, South Carolina, Tennessee, Rhode Island, New Mexico, Colorado, and Oklahoma. Specifically, the NPP received favorable court decisions in several major prison conditions cases, including: *Pugh* v. *Locke* (Alabama, 1976, successfully challenged the "totality of conditions" in Alabama state prisons as being constitutionally inadequate); gleaned consent decrees in cases such as *Brown* v. *Murray* (Virginia maximum security facility, in 1985), and *Spear* v. *Ariyoshi* (Hawaii prisons, 1985). NPP representatives frequently offer testimony before Congress and sponsor numerous educational programs and seminars for law students and lawyers. The NPP is active on other penal fronts such as "behavior modification," AIDS in prisons, alternatives to incarceration, and publicizing information on states currently under court order to reduce their prison populations.

FURTHER INFORMATION/RESOURCES

The NPP publishes the *National Prison Project Journal*, quarterly; the *Status Report on the Courts and the Prisons*, annually; and the *Prisoner's Assistance Directory*, which lists and describes organizations devoted to helping prisoners, annually.

Reference

National Prison Project of the ACLU. (1990). *The National Prison Project Journal: A Project of the American Civil Liberties Union Foundation, Inc.* Washington, DC: American Civil Liberties Union.

NATIONAL PROBATION AND PAROLE ASSOCIATION
See National Council on Crime and Delinquency.

NATIONAL PROBATION ASSOCIATION
See National Council on Crime and Delinquency.

NATIONAL RIFLE ASSOCIATION/INSTITUTE FOR LEGISLATIVE ACTION (NRA, NRA-ILA)
1600 Rhode Island Avenue, NW
P.O. Box 90087
Washington, DC 20090–0087
(800) 368–5714

ORGANIZATIONAL HISTORY/DEVELOPMENT

Established in 1871, the National Rifle Association (NRA) has been called "the most effective special interest group in Washington" (James A. Inciardi, *Criminal Justice* [San Francisco, CA: Academic Press, Inc., 1984], p. 764). With over 2.5 million members, a full-time staff of 400, and annual budget of

$90 million, the National Rifle Association is certainly the leading pro-gun special interest group in the country. Originally organized as a militia-related organization in the mid-1800s, and developing into a group concerned with wildlife management and conservation in the mid/late-1800s, the organization today is concerned primarily with the legislative protection of rights of gun owners and hunters. In 1975 the NRA established it's Institute for Legislative Action (NRA-ILA), which is now the lobbying arm of the NRA (the NRA itself actually being the world's largest private gun club).

MISSION STATEMENT/PURPOSE

"To protect and defend the Constitution of the United States, especially with reference to the inalienable right of the individual American citizen guaranteed by such Constitution to acquire, possess, transport, carry, transfer ownership of, and enjoy the right to use arms, in order that the people may always be in a position to exercise their legitimate individual rights of self-preservation and defense of family, person, and property, as well as to serve effectively in the appropriate militia for the common defense of the Republic and the individual liberty of its citizens. A) To ensure a well-regulated militia, i.e., able-bodied citizens familiar with firearms, by encouraging those who might have to serve in the military to be familiar with rifles (handguns were added in 1866). B) To defend the Second Amendment to the U.S. Constitution and the right of the people to keep and bear arms for individual, family, and national defense, for hunting and target shooting, and other lawful purposes."

KEY POLICY ACTIVITY/CONCERNS

While being generally devoted to the preservation of the Second Amendment provision to "keep and bear arms," the NRA has supported mandatory sentences for criminals using firearms in the commission of crimes, instant telephone background checks on citizens purchasing firearms, and the right of private citizens to carry concealed weapons. The group is also strongly supportive of the rights of hunters and recreational target shooters, particularly with regards to the purchase and possession of semiautomatic assault rifles. The NRA had a significant impact on reform of the Gun Control Act of 1986 by its promotion of the Firearm Owners' Protection Act of 1986. The group has opposed so-called "waiting periods" for the purchase of firearms, however, with or without background checks, and restrictions on the use and purchase of firearms by "upstanding" (nonfelony-convicted) citizens generally. The NRA participates in all forms of lobbying including political action committees, campaign contributions, direct mailing, and extensive grassroots level activity nationwide. NRA positions on legislation are often considered important by many prospective legislative voters.

FURTHER INFORMATION/RESOURCES

The NRA publishes *The American Rifleman* and *The American Hunter*, both monthly magazines.

NATIONAL URBAN LEAGUE, INC.

References

Leddy, Edward F. (1987). *Magnum Force Lobby: The National Rifle Association Fights Gun Control*. Lanham, MD: University Press of America.
Sugarmann, Josh. (1992). *National Rifle Association: Money, Firepower and Fear*. Washington, DC: National Press Books.
Trefethen, James B., compiler, and James E. Serven, editor. (1967). *Americans and Their Guns; The National Rifle Association Story Through Nearly a Century of Service to the Nation*. Harrisburg, PA: Stackpole Books.

NATIONAL SOCIETY OF STATE LEGISLATORS
See National Conference of State Legislators.

NATIONAL URBAN LEAGUE, INC. (NUL)
John E. Jacob, Chief Executive Officer
500 E. 62nd Street
New York, NY 10021
(212) 310–9000

ORGANIZATIONAL HISTORY/DEVELOPMENT

"Founded in 1910, the National Urban League (NUL) is the premier social service and civil rights organization in America. The League is a nonprofit, nonpartisan community-based organization with 12 affiliates in 34 states and the District of Columbia. The NUL is governed by an interracial Board of Trustees composed of outstanding men and women from the professions, business, labor, civic [and] religious communities" (from National Urban League, *FACT SHEET*, 1992).

MISSION STATEMENT/PURPOSE

"To assist African Americans in the achievement of social and economic equality. The League implements its mission through advocacy, bridge building, program services, and research."

KEY POLICY ACTIVITY/CONCERNS

The National Urban League has most recently developed its "Marshall Plan for America" in response to the 1992 urban riots occurring in Los Angeles and other American cities. This plan advocates massive reinvestment in America's inner cities and the establishment of minority-oriented job training and investment programs. This organization has a long history of activism on issues ranging from poverty and urban decline to economic racism in credit and employment practices to civil rights issues generally. The NUL is the foremost organization promoting the civil rights of African-American citizens in the United States.

FURTHER INFORMATION/RESOURCES

The major publications of the National Urban League are *The National Urban League Review*, the *Quarterly Economic Report on the African American Worker*, and *Runta: The National Urban League Research Department Fact Sheet*. Two recent editions of the *National Urban League Review* were titled "Racism in America: The Continuing Struggle of African Americans," and "African American Issues in the Nineties: Cause for Alarm and Action." The NUL publishes numerous additional pamphlets and monographs on various topics.

NORTH AMERICAN ASSOCIATION OF WARDENS AND SUPERINTENDENTS (NAAWS)
c/o Mr. O'Sullivan
150 27th Street W.
Prince Albert, SK
Canada S6V 5E5
(306) 763-0772

ORGANIZATIONAL HISTORY/DEVELOPMENT

Established in 1870 and formerly titled the Wardens Association of America (1971) and the American Association of Wardens and Superintendents (1980), this private, nonprofit organization is comprised of wardens, superintendents, and other executives of correctional facilities throughout the country. With over 250 members divided into five regional groups, the North American Association of Wardens and Superintendents (NAAWS) seeks to facilitate communication among correctional executives and to improve the administration of jails and prisons.

MISSION STATEMENT/PURPOSE

"To focus national attention on the problems and programs of correctional institutions and to promote better management of these institutions."

KEY POLICY ACTIVITY/CONCERNS

The NAAWS grants the National Warden of the Year Award, assists states upon request in the evaluation of prison standards, and holds semiannual meetings in conjunction with the American Correctional Association.[*]

FURTHER INFORMATION/RESOURCES

The NAAWS publishes *The Grapevine*, a bimonthly newsletter.

NORTH AMERICAN JUDGES ASSOCIATION
See American Judges Association.

P

———————————— / ————————————

PACT INSTITUTE OF JUSTICE (PIJ)
254 S. Morgan Boulevard
Valparaiso, IN 46383
(219) 462–1127

ORGANIZATIONAL HISTORY/DEVELOPMENT

No information.

MISSION STATEMENT/PURPOSE

No information.

KEY POLICY ACTIVITY/CONCERNS

Working in collaboration with the Mennonite Church (see Mennonite Central Committee*), the PACT Institute for Justice (PIJ) has been a national leader in the development of Victim-Offender Reconciliation/Mediation Programs (''VORPs'' or ''VOMPs''). These programs seek to bring victims and offenders together in order to give the victim a chance to speak to the offender (which almost never occurs in the criminal justice system) and also to attempt to reconcile the two parties. This approach views crime as a violation of community trust and seeks to restore relationships broken by crime. Victim Offender Mediation/Reconciliation Programs are seldom used for violent crimes but have become an increasingly popular option for the resolution of minor property and juvenile offenses. By giving the two parties a chance to work things out themselves, these programs seek to reduce the divisiveness of the adversarial process.

FURTHER INFORMATION/RESOURCES

The PIJ publishes handbooks, pamphlets, and workbooks designed to assist in the training of mediators and in the organization of mediation sessions. PACT's *The VORP Handbook* is widely used throughout the country.

PENNSYLVANIA CRIME COMMISSION (PCC)
1100 E. Hector Street, Suite 470
Conshohocken, PA 19428
(215) 834–1164

ORGANIZATIONAL HISTORY/DEVELOPMENT

The Pennsylvania Crime Commission (PCC) was founded in response to a recommendation of the President's Crime Commission (1967) that states with organized crime groups create independent, permanent crime commissions to investigate and report on organized crime. In 1978, the Pennsylvania State Legislature restructured PCC as an independent state agency, granting it autonomy from the executive branch of state government.

MISSION STATEMENT/PURPOSE

"The PCC operates in response to a legislative mandate charging it with the task of investigating and reporting on the nature and scope of organized crime and political corruption in Pennsylvania."

KEY POLICY ACTIVITY/CONCERNS

Investigates and develops intelligence on organized crime in Pennsylvania; publishes an annual report on the nature and scope of organized crime and political corruption in that state; and provides training for federal, state, and local law enforcement officials in Pennsylvania.

FURTHER INFORMATION/RESOURCES

In 1970 the PCC published its *Report on Organized Crime*; in 1980, *Report on Organized Crime*; and in 1990, *Report on Organized Crime: A Decade of Change*.

PEOPLE ORGANIZED TO STOP RAPE OF IMPRISONED PERSONS (POSRIP)
Tom Cahill, Executive Director
P.O. Box 632
Ft. Bragg, CA 95437
(707) 964–2138

ORGANIZATIONAL HISTORY/DEVELOPMENT

People Organized to Stop Rape of Imprisoned Persons (POSRIP) was founded in 1979 by Russell D. Smith as a private, nonprofit organization devoted to giving voice to the problems of prison rape and to initiating a support group for prison rape victims. POSRIP has roughly twenty-five members (active and inactive), an annual budget of less than $1,000, and seeks correspondents for victims of prison rape.

MISSION STATEMENT/PURPOSE

"To raise awareness of the occurrence of barbaric rape in prisons, to monitor prison rape, and to act as a support group for survivors."

KEY POLICY ACTIVITY/CONCERNS

POSRIP is devoted to protecting inmates' Eighth Amendment rights securing them from "cruel and unusual punishments" as well as their Thirteenth Amendment rights protecting them from slavery. POSRIP views the condition of American prisons as those that foster both cruel and unusual punishment and sexual slavery. The organization suggests that inhumane conditions in prisons foster further criminal activity in inmates upon release and is particularly concerned with the problem of sexual slavery and forced prostitution in prisons. AIDS in prisons and the raping of inmates by guards as punishment for misbehavior is also a central concern of the group. The organization attempts to collect statistics on occurrences of prison rape in order to provide evidence of "cruel and unusual" punishment. The group maintains, however, that incentive to report rape in prison is absent, since doing so can lead to further victimization. The group has lobbied legislators and sponsored a direct mailing drive.

FURTHER INFORMATION/RESOURCES

POSRIP publishes a newsletter and occasional magazine articles on the impact of prison rape on inmates.

PRESBYTERIAN CRIMINAL JUSTICE PROGRAM (PCJP), SOCIAL JUSTICE AND PEACEMAKING MINISTRY UNIT

Reverand Kathy Lancaster
Presbyterian Criminal Justice Program
Social Justice and Peacemaking Ministry Unit
100 Witherspoon Street, Room 3044
Louisville, KY 40202
(502) 569–5803

ORGANIZATIONAL HISTORY/DEVELOPMENT

No information.

MISSION STATEMENT/PURPOSE

"To work to bring together the religious community and the criminal justice system; to base its work on General Assembly policies in areas related to the criminal justice system; to work for the church's increased involvement in ministry with victims of crime, prisoners, former prisoners, juveniles and others in the system; to provide resources and networking opportunities for prison chaplains, direct-service providers, advocates for change and other interested people;

to work toward the development of alternatives to prison through church-based organizations.''

KEY POLICY ACTIVITY/CONCERNS

Acting through the General Assembly of the Presbyterian Church (U.S.A.), the Presbyterian Criminal Justice Program (PCJP) publishes position papers on virtually every controversial criminal justice issue, ranging from the death penalty to gun control to privacy issues and legal aid. One of the most articulate of the ''religiously based'' criminal justice interest groups, PCJP has integrated criminal justice issues into the fabric of its operational function. The organization sponsors its ''Beyond Fear'' workshops, which seek to enhance peaceful responses to conflict in communities and to reduce fear of crime.

FURTHER INFORMATION/RESOURCES

The PCJP publishes an annual newsletter, *Justice Jottings*, in February and numerous position papers and manuscripts, including *Restorative Justice: Toward Nonviolence*; *Juvenile Justice: Involvement for Christians*; *Hope, Respect, Reconciliation: A Christian Response to Gun Violence*; ''Young People and the Death Penalty,'' a position paper on that issue and many others.

PRISON-ASHRAM PROJECT (of the Human Kindness Foundation)
Bo Lozoff, Director
Route 1, Box 201–N
Durham, NC 27705
(919) 942–2138

ORGANIZATIONAL HISTORY/DEVELOPMENT

Established in 1973 as a private, nonprofit organization devoted to developing and nurturing the spiritual life of prisoners by educating them about the spiritual possibilities of their confinement, the Prison-Ashram Project seeks to reduce the level of violence in prisons and in society. While no longer active inside the prisons, the Prison-Ashram Project continues to make available informational literature and resources to inmates who ask for them.

MISSION STATEMENT/PURPOSE

''To offer prisoners and others a free, down-to-earth spiritual resource through correspondence, books, workshops and newsletters.''

KEY POLICY ACTIVITY/CONCERNS

The Prison-Ashram Project encourages prisoners and other shut-ins to develop and nurture their spirituality by utilizing their confinement in constructive ways. (Ashram refers to a Hindu monastic tradition that encourages a life of simplicity and spiritual devotion.)

FURTHER INFORMATION/RESOURCES

Publications of the Prison-Ashram Project include *We're All Doing Time*; *Lineage and Other Stories*, and many other pamphlets, audiocassettes, and books—which are all made available cheaply to inmates.

PRISON FELLOWSHIP
See Justice Fellowship.

PRISON RESEARCH EDUCATION ACTION PROGRAM
See Safer Society Program.

PRISONERS' RIGHTS UNION (PRU)
2300 J Street
P.O. Box 1019
Sacramento, CA 95812–1019
(916) 441–4214

ORGANIZATIONAL HISTORY/DEVELOPMENT

The Prisoners' Rights Union (PRU) was founded in 1971 as a private, nonprofit organization in the aftermath of a prison strike at Folsom prison (California) with three major goals: (1) the abolition of indeterminate sentencing; (2) the restoration of civil rights for prisoners; and (3) the payment of a living wage to prisoners for all work done in prisons. The PRU currently has about 12,000 members, a full-time staff of six (plus forty-five volunteers), and an annual budget of $100,000. The Prisoners' Rights Union is one of the most active prisoners' rights groups in the United States.

MISSION STATEMENT/PURPOSE

"To improve conditions for prisoners in California prisons and jails and to educate the public about penal issues. To influence the government to avoid over-reliance on incarceration and to educate prisoners and their families about their rights."

KEY POLICY ACTIVITY/CONCERNS

The PRU has filed thirteen lawsuits against the state of California regarding prisoners' rights issues and publishes the nation's first and largest prison newspaper. In fact, much of the PRU's litigation has involved establishing the right of "freedom of expression" in prisons via inmate newspapers. PRU moved from San Francisco to Sacramento, California, in 1988. The group is active in prisoners' rights legislative initiatives and plays an active role in resolving convict grievances in the California prison system.

FURTHER INFORMATION/RESOURCES

The PRU publishes a newspaper, *The California Prisoner*, with 9,000 subscribers, the *California State Prisoner's Handbook*, and the *California Prisoner's Resource Guide*.

Q
/

QUAKER COMMITTEE ON JAILS AND JUSTICE (QCJJ)
60 Lowther Avenue
Toronto, Ontario
Canada M5R 1C7

ORGANIZATIONAL HISTORY/DEVELOPMENT

The Quaker Committee on Jails and Justice (QCJJ) was founded in 1975 as a private, nonprofit organization devoted to prison reform. The organization has since established a national committee and its Canadian Chapter of the Alternatives to Violence Project. The organization also has formed a committee on restorative justice. The QCJJ currently has over 1,000 members and an annual budget of about $25,000 (Canadian). For more information on Quaker involvement in the criminal justice system, see American Friends Service Committee.*

MISSION STATEMENT/PURPOSE

"To provide support and structure for friends interested in criminal justice and community issues."

KEY POLICY ACTIVITY/CONCERNS

The Quaker Committee on Jails and Justice encourages prison visitation, reintegration of offenders into the community, teaching alternatives to violence, prisoner advocacy, and establishing alternatives to incarceration. The Quakers are widely known for their desire to abolish the use of prisons as a response to crime and have a long tradition of criminal justice involvement. The Quakers, long known for their pacifism, are also opposed to the death penalty.

FURTHER INFORMATION/RESOURCES

No information provided.

S

—————————— / ——————————

SAFER SOCIETY PROGRAM (SSP)
Faye Honey Knopp, Executive Director
RR1 Box 24–B
Orwell, VT 05760–9756
(802) 897–7541

ORGANIZATIONAL HISTORY/DEVELOPMENT

Founded in 1972 and formerly titled Prison Research Education Action Program, the Safer Society Program (SSP) was designed "to bring about a safer society by reducing imprisonment and increasing restorative processes for victims and offenders." The organization is presently engaged primarily in bringing about alternative responses to sex crimes. SSP currently has a staff of six.

MISSION STATEMENT/PURPOSE

"Sponsored by the New York State Council of Churches to provide a national research, advocacy, and referral center for the prevention of sexual abuse, the SSP is perhaps the leading private criminal justice organization devoted to the issue of sex abuse and sex crime."

KEY POLICY ACTIVITY/CONCERNS

Safer Society Program representatives have presented testimony before legislative bodies, engaged in lobbying and direct mailing, and have sponsored numerous educational and training programs. SSP has been opposed to mandatory sentencing schemes and the death penalty. In addition, the organization serves as a major clearinghouse/resource/networking center for newly emerging organizations devoted to sex abuse and crime. The SSP also facilitates speakers and numerous informational seminars on topics related to sex crimes and abuse. The Safer Society Program has established a national referral service for sex offender treatment and is currently publishing the first self-help workbook for sex offenders. SSP has also provided offender-prevention programming in public schools.

FURTHER INFORMATION/RESOURCES

The SSP publishes many pamphlets, workbooks, and books including *Instead of Prisons: A Handbook for Abolitionists* via its Safer Society Press.

THE SENTENCING PROJECT
918 F Street, NW, Suite 501
Washington, DC 20004
(202) 628–0871

ORGANIZATIONAL HISTORY/DEVELOPMENT

The Sentencing Project was founded in 1986 as a private, nonprofit organization intended to develop sentencing programs that promote alternatives to incarceration and to help the criminal justice system better meet the needs of indigent defendants. The organization maintains that the typical inmate in America's prisons is the "indigent felony client of public defenders and assigned council." The Sentencing Project seeks to remedy the unequal justice afforded indigents and is actually a combined effort of the National Council on Crime and Delinquency.*

MISSION STATEMENT/PURPOSE

"In coordination with the National Legal Aid and Defender Association (NLADA) and the National Council on Crime and Delinquency (NCCD), the Sentencing Project seeks to develop sentencing programs designed to promote alternatives to incarceration and to improve the sentencing of indigent defendants."

KEY POLICY ACTIVITY/CONCERNS

The Sentencing Project designs and introduces sentencing programs into state and local court systems in numerous jurisdictions nationwide. For example, the Sentencing Project has initiated alternative sentencing programs in over thirty jurisdictions in thirteen states, with one program in North Carolina becoming the model for eighteen other state-funded North Carolina programs. The group works primarily with defense attorneys and calls its approach to sentencing "defense-based," due to the unusually high level at which defense attorneys participate in the establishment of the project's sentencing schemes. Representatives and staff of the Sentencing Project are frequently called upon to testify before congressional committees, and they also provide technical assistance and consulting services to numerous criminal justice agencies at the national, state, and local levels.

FURTHER INFORMATION/RESOURCES

Two prominent publications of the Sentencing Project are reports published upon completion of research projects: "Young Black Men and the Criminal Justice System: A Growing National Problem" and "Americans Behind Bars: A Comparison of International Rates of Incarceration."

SHANTI PROJECT
525 Howard Street
San Francisco, CA 94105–3080
(415) 777–CARE

ORGANIZATIONAL HISTORY/DEVELOPMENT

The SHANTI Project was founded in 1974 as a private, nonprofit organization devoted to the care of the terminally ill, and now, with the onset of the AIDS epidemic, has devoted its full attention to the care of persons with AIDS and their loved ones. The SHANTI Project currently has over 700 volunteer workers in San Francisco and an annual budget of $4.2 million.

MISSION STATEMENT/PURPOSE

"SHANTI Project is a volunteer-based, nonprofit organization serving people with AIDS, people with severe or disabling disease, and their loved ones. SHANTI Project provides emotional, practical, residential, social, and other support services to people with HIV disease living in San Francisco. Its mission is helping people to live with issues related to HIV disease and to enhance and maximize the quality of their lives."

KEY POLICY ACTIVITY/CONCERNS

The SHANTI Project is first and foremost devoted to providing services and care for persons with AIDS at the city and local level. In recent years, however, the organization has placed increasing emphasis on AIDS policy issues at the national level. SHANTI Project orchestrates support groups, peer counseling, practical assistance like transportation, and long-term, low-cost housing to eligible individuals with AIDS. The group also offers psychosocial training programs to health care professionals, clergy, and laypersons who are interested in the special problems AIDS and HIV-positive status bring about, that is, loss of health insurance, loss of job, and often the loss of friends and family through stigmatization. SHANTI Project makes available a series of fifteen videotapes to interested organizations and acts as a model for future potential care givers. It is believed that SHANTI Project may effectively serve as an information resource in response to the growing problem of HIV/AIDS in the nation's prisons.

FURTHER INFORMATION/RESOURCES

The SHANTI Project publishes *Eclipse*, a quarterly newsletter; the *People with AIDS Newsletter* and the *Volunteer Newsletter*, each monthly.

SOCIETY FOR THE ADVANCEMENT OF CRIMINOLOGY
See American Society of Criminology.

(SOCIETY OF THE) TRANSFIGURATION PRISON MINISTRIES (TPM)
James Yeager, Editor
c/o Sister Evelyn Ancilla, C.T., Director
495 Albion Avenue, Glendale
Cincinnati, OH 45246
(513) 771–5291
(800) 488–5743

ORGANIZATIONAL HISTORY/DEVELOPMENT

Founded in 1975 with the writing of a few Christmas cards to inmates at local prisons, Transfiguration Prison Ministries (TPM) now assists over 2,000 inmates via correspondence and personal resources (e.g., monies for personal goods like toothpaste). TPM is supported by the Society of the Transfiguration, a Catholic order of nuns devoted to community service.

MISSION STATEMENT/PURPOSE

"To give information about prisoners and prison/judicial systems to readers both incarcerated and in society."

KEY POLICY ACTIVITY/CONCERNS

The primary activity of TPM is in the provision of "care packages" to needy inmates and the facilitation of correspondence between inmates and community members. The organization also publishes a seasonal newsletter devoted to discussing prison issues.

FURTHER INFORMATION/RESOURCES

Society of the Transfiguration Prison Ministries publishes a quarterly newsletter, *Transfiguration Prison Ministry*, and *Transfiguration Quarterly*.

U

———————— / ————————

UNITARIAN UNIVERSALIST ASSOCIATION OF CONGREGATIONS
WASHINGTON OFFICE FOR SOCIAL JUSTICE (UUACOSJ)
100 Maryland Avenue, NE, Room 106
Washington, DC 20002
(202) 547–0254

ORGANIZATIONAL HISTORY/DEVELOPMENT

No information.

MISSION STATEMENT/PURPOSE

No information.

KEY POLICY ACTIVITY/CONCERNS

The UUACOSJ actively supported the National Moratorium on Prison Construction and has supported the abolition of the death penalty in coordination with Amnesty International USA* and the American Friends Service Committee,* among many others. Recently the Unitarian Universalist Association accepted into its membership a congregation made up entirely of inmates held at a medium-security prison in New Mexico. This self-governing congregation is the 1,001st congregation of the Unitarian Universalist Association in North America. The Unitarian Universalist Church has been active in a wide range of criminal justice issues.

FURTHER INFORMATION/RESOURCES

The UUACOSJ publishes numerous position papers on criminal justice issues such as the death penalty, alternatives to incarceration, and prison overcrowding.

U.S. CATHOLIC CONFERENCE (USCC)
3211 4th Street, NE
Washington, DC 20017
(202) 541–3000

ORGANIZATIONAL HISTORY/DEVELOPMENT

Established in 1919 as a private, nonprofit organization devoted to the service of the American Catholic Bishops Association, the U.S. Catholic Conference (USCC) was formed out of the earlier National Catholic Welfare Council (1923) and the National Catholic Welfare Conference (1966); the organization absorbed the National Center on Religious Education in 1976. The USCC currently has a staff of 400 and an annual budget of over $30 million.

MISSION STATEMENT/PURPOSE

"To assist the American Catholic Bishops in their service to the church in this country by uniting the people of God where voluntary, collective action on a broad diocesan level is needed."

KEY POLICY ACTIVITY/CONCERNS

The USCC has actively opposed the use of the death penalty in the United States and around the world and has advocated the abolition of this punishment. Stating that since "racist attitudes and the social consequences of racism have some influence in determining who is sentenced to die in our society," the USCC does not regard the punishment as acceptable. The formal position of the church regarding punishment in general is that "it is the social responsibility of the Church to provide a community of faith and trust in which God's grace can heal the personal and spiritual wounds caused by crime and in which we can all grow by sharing one another's burdens and sorrows."

FURTHER INFORMATION/RESOURCES

The USCC publishes *USCC Currents*, a monthly newsletter, and *Pastoral Ministry*, a series.

THE U.S. CONFERENCE OF MAYORS (USCM)
1620 I Street, NW
Washington, DC 20006
(202) 293–7330

ORGANIZATIONAL HISTORY/DEVELOPMENT

Founded in 1932 as a private, nonprofit organization the U.S. Conference of Mayors (USCM) was designed to establish a direct relationship between the federal government and the cities to influence the development of national public policy on the cities' behalf. The USCM represents the over 1,000 cities in the United States with populations over 30,000. In 1949, the USCM heavily influenced the passage of the Housing Act of 1949. In 1986 the organization assisted in the passage of the Community Block Grant Program, the Anti-Drug Abuse Act, the Urban Development Action Program, and other key urban programs. The USCM is a very influential organization with regard to issues of criminal justice and offers frequent position papers, policy statements, and congressional testimony on numerous issues. The organization has a full-time staff of between forty-five and fifty, depending on seasonal workload.

MISSION STATEMENT/PURPOSE

"To influence and develop national public policy and provide information and assistance to mayors and other public officials."

KEY POLICY ACTIVITY/CONCERNS

The key activities of the USCM are lobbying, technical assistance and research projects, the holding of annual meetings, and the issuing of policy statements that reflect the views of the majority of the nation's mayors. The USCM has supported the "Brady Bill," a gun-control initiative sponsored by former press secretary Jim Brady, who was injured in the assassination attempt on President Reagan in 1981. Most recently, in the wake of the 1992 Los Angeles riots, the USCM has been active in addressing the problems of inner-city violence. The organization has a long history of policy activity, however, including the establishment of general revenue sharing policies and the development and orchestration of numerous Community Development Block Grants over the years. The group has also strongly supported limitations on the purchase and possession of hand guns for urban residents. The USCM has participated in the passage of the Anti-Drug Abuse Act of 1986 and other key urban programs.

FURTHER INFORMATION/RESOURCES

The USCM publishes an *Annual Report* and numerous special issue position papers.

V

/

VERA INSTITUTE OF JUSTICE (VIJ)
Michael E. Smith, Director
377 Broadway, 11th Floor
New York, NY 10013
(212) 334–1300

ORGANIZATIONAL HISTORY/DEVELOPMENT

Established in 1961 as a private, nonprofit organization designed to work in the area of criminal justice reform, particularly in the area of postrelease job placement for inmates, the Vera Institute of Justice (VIJ) has become one of the nation's largest criminal justice research organizations. In its early days, the Vera Institute (then the "Vera Foundation," named after the mother of Vera's founder, New York industrialist Louis Schweitzer) was active in the establishment of pretrial release programs and other bail reform efforts (James A. Inciardi, *Criminal Justice* [San Francisco, CA: Harcourt Brace Jovanovich, 1987], p. 405). The Manhattan Bail Project was launched by Schweitzer in 1961, who believed that "more persons can successfully be released . . . if verified information concerning their character and roots in the community is available to the court at the time of bail determination"(ibid.). A variation of the Manhattan Bail Project is still being administered by the New York City Criminal Justice Agency. In recent years, the VIJ has placed an increasing emphasis on victim's rights programs via its New York City Victim Services Agency.

At present the VIJ has a full-time staff of over 200 (this varies by project and funding) and an annual budget of roughly $15 million. Much of the organization's funding comes from contract work with the U.S. Department of Justice, where the institute's programs are largely directed at employment and homelessness issues for released inmates.

MISSION STATEMENT/PURPOSE

"Seeks to aid in the administration and development of community sentencing programs and in the establishment of viable employment opportunities for non-violent, non-habitual criminals."

KEY POLICY ACTIVITY/CONCERNS

The VIJ is among the most active of criminal justice agencies in the country, administering numerous U.S. Department of Justice community block grants and work release programs, among other contract work. A typical example of the kind of program the institute is known for is the "Day Fine Program" in Bridgeport, Connecticut. This program, along with similar programs like it across the country which VIJ helped administer, offers judges an alternative sentencing scheme for nonviolent, often indigent, offenders in the form of a fine. This fine is levied according to the defendant's ability to pay rather than simply on the severity of the crime—which is all taken in the context of the defendant's familial and other financial obligations. "The sanctions are referred to as 'Day Fines' because a defendant's daily wages are used to help calculate the penalty" (Rosemary P. McNicholas, "Criminal Fines: From Each According to His Ability to Pay," *The Connecticut Law Tribune*, January 13, 1992, p. 3). The program is said to have offered flexibility to judges in sentencing and assisted defendants by allowing them to pay fines on an installment basis—keeping low-income offenders out of jail for failure to pay and reducing costs.

FURTHER INFORMATION/RESOURCES

The VIJ has published numerous research reports including *Further Work in Criminal Justice Reform: 1971–1976* and *Felony Arrest: Their Prosecution and Disposition in New York City's Courts*. The organization also publishes a semiannual journal titled the *Federal Sentencing Reporter*, devoted to sentencing issues at the federal level.

Reference

Strasburg, Paul A. (1978). *Violent Delinquents: A Report to the Ford Foundation from the Vera Institute of Justice*. New York: Monarch Press.

W

---/---

WARDEN'S ASSOCIATION OF AMERICA
See North American Association of Wardens and Superintendents.

WE CARE PROGRAM, INC.
Route #2, Box 33–M
Atmore, AL 36502
(205) 368–8818

ORGANIZATIONAL HISTORY/DEVELOPMENT

Founded in 1984 as a private, nonprofit organization devoted to the pastoral care of inmates and their families, the We Care Program, Inc. works primarily in Alabama. In 1985, We Care Program, Inc. was endorsed by Associate Commissioner of Corrections for the state of Alabama, Tom L. Allen, and given wide access to Alabama prisoners. The We Care Program, Inc. currently has a staff of seventeen and an annual budget of over $350,000.

MISSION STATEMENT/PURPOSE

"We Care Program is an interdenominational organization consisting of Christian men and women who share a burden for and commitment to helping offenders and their families. Our purpose is to serve God, our society, and our Churches through programs which will present and interpret the truths of the Gospel to prison inmates and other offenders in order that the whole person will find new life and that the pattern of failure and crime will be replaced with patterns of success and productivity."

KEY POLICY ACTIVITY/CONCERNS

The We Care Program, Inc. works in coordination with the Alabama Department of Corrections, providing 30,000 hours per year in assistance free of charge to that organization. In addition, the We Care Program, Inc. recently became a formal (optional) segment of prisoner orientation in Alabama state prisons. The organization maintains an instructional video library that is made available to prisoners. We Care Program, Inc. also provides literacy training services and limited counseling to inmates.

FURTHER INFORMATION/RESOURCES

No information available.

WE TIP, INC.
P.O. Box 1296
Rancho Cucamonga, CA 91729–1296
(714) 987–5005
(800) 78–CRIME
(800) 47–ARSON

ORGANIZATIONAL HISTORY/DEVELOPMENT

Established in 1972 as a private, nonprofit organization devoted to crime prevention and detection through encouraging "anonymous tips," WE TIP, INC. started out in California with the establishment of a "drug-tip" phone line. By 1977 the organization maintained phone lines for all major crimes and had assisted in the arrest and conviction of dozens of criminals. In 1982 the organization was featured on an ABC television network program titled: "Counterattack: Crime in America." The organization now has a full-time staff of fifty-three, an annual budget of close to $1 million, and over 17,000 members.

MISSION STATEMENT/PURPOSE

"To be the most effective citizen crime reporting resource in our nation."

KEY POLICY ACTIVITY/CONCERNS

WE TIP, INC. sponsors the Eyewitness Anonymous Program and works with the news media to publicize various crimes. The organization's primary activity is the passing on of information gleaned by citizens to law enforcement regarding criminal activity. The group offers rewards of up to $1,000 for information relayed to law enforcement that result in convictions.

FURTHER INFORMATION/RESOURCES

WE TIP, INC. publishes numerous informational pamphlets, among them *WE TIP Crimebusters*, a monthly magazine; *WE TIP Crimeline*, a quarterly newspaper; and *WE TIP's National Crimefighter*, also a periodical.

WOMEN AGAINST RAPE (WAR)
P.O. Box 02084
Columbus, OH 43202
(614) 291–9751

ORGANIZATIONAL HISTORY/DEVELOPMENT

Founded in 1972 as a private, nonprofit organization devoted to preventing rape against women, Women Against Rape (WAR) sponsors a rape hotline and trains crisis intervention counselors. WAR currently has sixty-two active members and a subscription list of over 5,000.

MISSION STATEMENT/PURPOSE

Not available.

KEY POLICY ACTIVITY/CONCERNS

''Women Against Rape sponsors a victim assistance program and rape survivor support groups. WAR also stresses rape prevention tactics and actively sponsors self-defense classes for women. WAR also monitors national events relevant to the issue of rape and keeps members and subscribers appraised via its quarterly newsletter.''

FURTHER INFORMATION/RESOURCES

Women Against Rape publish the quarterly *W.A.R. Newsletter*.

WOMEN'S PRISON ASSOCIATION (WPA)
Ann Jacobs, Executive Director
110 2nd Avenue
New York, NY 10003
(212) 674–1163

ORGANIZATIONAL HISTORY/DEVELOPMENT

Founded in 1844 as a private, nonprofit organization devoted to meeting the needs of female prisoners, the Women's Prison Association (WPA) is the oldest American organization devoted strictly to the needs of women inmates. The organization currently has a staff of thirty-five and an annual budget of over $1 million.

MISSION STATEMENT/PURPOSE

''To provide direct services to women involved with or formerly involved with the criminal justice system. To provide transitional services to women coming out of prison.''

KEY POLICY ACTIVITY/CONCERNS

The Women's Prison Association provides services to women inmates by specifically offering assistance with counseling, education, legal advocacy, as well as transitional services for women released from prison. A particular concern of the WPA lies in meeting the special needs of women inmates who have children. The organization utilizes a foster care prevention program and rehabilitation and drug-use counseling to assist mothers who have come into contact with the criminal justice system. The organization makes a strong case for the fact that the needs of female prisoners are overlooked in the criminal justice system, which is devoted almost solely to the needs of men, and has asserted that women are the fastest-growing prison population. The WPA has supported alternatives to incarceration and has been particularly concerned about the occurrence of single-mother/child drug dependency. The distinctive needs of single mothers who often have no outside support have made many of them more vulnerable to the economic incentives of the drug trade. The WPA therefore sponsors a court diversion program for single mothers.

FURTHER INFORMATION/RESOURCES

No information available.

Y

————————————— / —————————————

YOKEFELLOWSHIP INTERNATIONAL PRISON MINISTRIES (YIPM)
1200 Almond Street
Williamsport, PA 17701
(212) 674–1163

ORGANIZATIONAL HISTORY/DEVELOPMENT

Founded in 1986 and formerly titled National Yokefellow Prison Ministry (1969) and Yokefellowship of Pennsylvania, Yokefellowship International Prison Ministries (YIPM) is a private, nonprofit organization devoted to prison ministry. With 2,500 members nationwide, YIPM has a long history of religious prison activism. YIPM has an annual budget of about $30,000 and a staff of two.

MISSION STATEMENT/PURPOSE

"To help serve the Christian and spiritual needs of residents in correctional and penal institutions; to bridge the gulf between persons confined in prisons and those in the outside community; to demonstrate a continuing concern for offenders in the process of reintegration into society and the Christian community; to promote and cooperate in the establishment and operation of local community-sponsored 'half-way' house facilities; to minister to persons on probation and those confined in city and county jails, state prisons, and federal institutions, and to provide support and fellowship to those involved in services to such persons; to initiate cooperative efforts to meet the needs of inmates and their families; to show concern for decisions made by those responsible for the policies and procedures of correctional institutions."

KEY POLICY ACTIVITY/CONCERNS

YIPM maintains a 5,000-volume library on religious and criminal justice related topics that is made available to prisoners and supervises training of prison ministers. The organization sponsors training sessions for lay-prison ministers and provides spiritual reading material to prisoners free of charge.

FURTHER INFORMATION/RESOURCES

YIPM publishes *Prison Ministry Yoke News*, quarterly, and the *Yokefellowship Prison Ministry Directory*, annually.

APPENDIX A: SURVEY QUESTIONNAIRE

————————— / —————————

INTRODUCTION

The information collected through this questionnaire will be used for a book describing criminal justice organizations and their public policy interests. The book will be published by Greenwood Press. We appreciate your help in providing answers to the questions.

INSTRUCTIONS

Please answer each question as completely as possible. If you do not know the answer to a question, skip it and go on to the next question.

Place the completed questionnaire in the self-addressed envelope and mail it back to us.

Thank you.

Part I   **NATURE AND ORIGIN OF YOUR ORGANIZATION**:

1.   Name of organization_____

      _____

2.   What year was it founded?   year_____

3.   What was the main reason why it was founded?_____

      _____

      _____

      _____

4.   What are a few of the milestones in the development of your
      organization?_____

      _____

      _____

      _____

      _____

      _____

5.   What are the goals of the organization?   (If there is a
      written mission statement, please include it)_____

      _____

      _____

      _____

6.   Have these goals changed over the years?   yes _____

                                                        no   _____

      If yes, how?_____

      _____

      _____

      _____

Part II **POLICY INTERESTS**:

7. Has your organization ever taken a position on legislation?

                                              yes _____

                                               no _____

                              (If no please skip to question #9)

8. What particular legislation did your organization support or
    oppose during the past two years and why?

         SUPPORT:_____

         _____

         _____

         _____

         OPPOSE:_____

         _____

         _____

         _____

9. On average, about how active would you say your organization
    is in trying to influence public policy?

         very   _____

         moderately   _____

         relatively little   _____

         not at all   _____

10. Which of the following strategies does your organization use
    in regard to public policy matters?

         Lobbying   _____

         Direct Mailing   _____

         Political Action Committees   _____

         Influencing Election Outcomes _____

         Other (Please specify)   _____

11. What level of government is most of your public policy
    activity aimed at?

         Federal   _____

         State   _____

         County   _____

         City   _____

12. Which organization besides yours would you say is the most
    prominent or effective in having an impact on policy matters
    in areas in which your organization is concerned? _____

    _____

    _____

13. How effective would you say your organization has been in
    getting changes in legislation that you want?

         very   _____

         moderate   _____

         relatively little   _____

         not at all   _____

Finally, a few questions about your organizational structure and
findings:

14. How many members does the organization have? #_____

15. Is this organization

         non profit   _____

         for profit   _____

16. Does it have a board of directors?

    yes   _____

    no   _____

17. Does it have a staff?

    yes   _____   # of staff ____

    no   _____

18. What is the organization's annual budget?

    $_____

19. What are the major sources of the organization's financial support?

                        <u>Approximate %</u>

    Corporate   _____

    Individual members _____

    Government   _____

    Foundations   _____

    Other (Please specify _____

20. Please describe briefly what the principal activities are that your organization engages in or sponsors_____

_____

_____

Thanks for your help.

APPENDIX B: STATISTICAL SUMMARY

————————————— / —————————————

QUESTION:

Have your organizational goals changed over the years?

Yes	41%
No	59%

Has your organization ever taken a position on legislation?

Percentage of organizations which had taken a position on legislation   66%

Percentage of organizations which had NOT taken a position on legislation   34%

On average, about how active would you say your organization is in trying to influence public policy?

Very	38%
Moderately	34%
Relatively little	16%
Not at all	12%

Which of the following strategies does your organization use in regard to public policy matters?

Lobbying	15%
Direct mail	13%
Political Action Committees	.02%
Other (please specify)	27%
Multiple strategies	44%

What level of government is most of your public policy activity aimed at?

Federal	27%
State	13%
County	0%
City	4%
Multiple	56%

How effective would you say your organization has been in getting changes in legislation that you want?

Very	18%
Moderately	47%
Relatively little	22%
Not at all	13%

Is this organization nonprofit or for profit?

Nonprofit	100%
For profit	0%

Does the organization have a board of directors?

Yes	100%
No	0%

Does the organization have a staff?

Yes	93%
No	7%

(___56%___) of organizations had a staff of five or less, while (___25%___) had ten or fewer.

Median number of organizational members: ___3170 members.___ ___79%___ of organizations, however, had membership of 5,000 or below, while only ___.02%___ had membership above 50,000.

Median annual budget for all organizations: ___$87,500.___ This category had a bimodal distribution, with organizations either having an annual budget of under $10,000 (___42%___) or an annual budget of higher than $5 million (___24%___).

Major sources of organization's funding support:

Corporate	8%
Individual members	48%
Government	16%

Foundations	.01%
Other	.06%
Multiple	28%

APPENDIX C: DIRECTORY OF GROUPS' REGULAR PUBLICATIONS

———————————— / ————————————

GENERAL

ABA Bankers Weekly (Weekly)—American Bankers Association

ACJS Today (quarterly)—Academy of Criminal Justice Sciences

The American Hunter (monthly)—National Rifle Association/Institute for Legislative Action

The American Rifleman (monthly)—National Rifle Association/Institute for Legislative Action

Amnesty Action (bimonthly)—Amnesty International USA

Amnesty International Report (annually)—Amnesty International USA

Annual Report (annually)—National Association for the Advancement of Colored People Legal Defense Fund

Annual Report (annually)—National Center for Youth Law

Bibliographic Guide for Prosecutors (annually)—National College of District Attorneys

Catalyst (10 times per year)—National Crime Prevention Council

Challenges and Opportunities in Drug Prevention: A Demand Reduction Resource Guide for Law Enforcement Officers—National Crime Prevention Council

The Champion—National Association of Criminal Defense Lawyers

Citizen's Guide to Marijuana Laws (seasonally)—National Organization for Reform of Marijuana Laws

CJS (quarterly)—American Bar Association Section of Criminal Justice

Commission Updates—Milton S. Eisenhower Foundation

CRAV (informational brochure)—Conflict Resolution/Alternatives to Violence

Crime and Delinquency—National Council on Crime and Delinquency

Criminal Organizations (before 1988 *Update*)—International Association for the Study of Organized Crime

The Criminologist (bimonthly)—American Society of Criminology

Criminology: An Interdisciplinary Journal (quarterly)—American Society of Criminology

Crisis (ten times per year)—National Association for the Advancement of Colored People Legal Defense Fund

Eclipse (quarterly)—SHANTI Project

FBI Petition News—National Committee Against Repressive Legislation

Federal Sentencing Reporter (semiannually)—Vera Institute of Justice

Felony Arrest: Their Prosecution and Disposition in New York City's Courts—Vera Institute of Justice

Fortune News (quarterly)—Fortune Society

Freedom to Act—National Committee Against Repressive Legislation

Further Work in Criminal Justice Reform: 1971–1976—Vera Institute of Justice

Guns Don't Die—People Do—Handgun Control, Inc.

The Gun Owner's Political Action Manual—Citizens Committee for the Right to Keep and Bear Arms

Handgun Control—Washington Report (quarterly)—Handgun Control, Inc.

INFORUM—National Council on Child Abuse and Family Violence

Ink & Airtime: Working Effectively with the Media—National Crime Prevention Council

Instead of Prisons: A Handbook for Abolitionists—Safer Society Program

Journal of Criminal Justice Education (semiannually)—Academy of Criminal Justice Sciences

Journal of Research in Crime and Delinquency—National Council on Crime and Delinquency

Journal of the American Criminal Justice Association (semiannually)—American Criminal Justice Association

Justice Bulletin (monthly)—National Criminal Justice Association

Justice Quarterly (quarterly)—Academy of Criminal Justice Sciences

Justice Research (bimonthly)—National Criminal Justice Association

Juvenile Court Statistics (annually)—National Center for Juvenile Justice

Juvenile Justice—National Criminal Justice Association

KINDEX: An Index to Periodical Literature Concerning Children (annually)—National Center for Juvenile Justice

Law and Social Inquiry (quarterly)—American Bar Foundation

The Leaflet (seasonally)—National Organization for Reform of Marijuana Laws

Legal Investigator (bimonthly)—National Association of Legal Investigators

Local Criminal Justice Issues Newsletter—National Association of Blacks in Criminal Justice

MADDvocate (twice per year)—Mothers Against Drunk Driving

MADD in Action (quarterly)—Mothers Against Drunk Driving

MADD National Newsletter—Mothers Against Drunk Driving

NABCJ Minority Criminal Justice Directory—National Association of Blacks in Criminal Justice

NABCJ Newsletter—National Association of Blacks in Criminal Justice

National Coalition Against Domestic Violence—Voice (quarterly)—National Coalition Against Domestic Violence

National Coalition Against Sexual Assault—Newsletter (quarterly)—National Coalition Against Sexual Assault

National Lawyers Guild—Guild Notes (bimonthly)—National Lawyers Guild

National Lawyers Guild—Guild Practitioner (quarterly)—National Lawyers Guild

National Lawyers Guild—Referral Directory (two times per year)—National Lawyers Guild

National Organization for Victim Assistance—Newsletter (monthly)—National Organization for Victim Assistance

The National Urban League Review—National Urban League Inc.

New Spirit (quarterly)—National Association of Town Watch

News Update (semimonthly)—National Association of Criminal Justice Planners

On Watch (bimonthly)—National Lawyer's Guild

Our Vanishing Freedom—Citizens Committee for the Right to Keep and Bear Arms

Oyez (ten times per year)—National College of District Attorneys

People with AIDS Newsletter (monthly)—SHANTI Project

Point Blank (monthly)—Citizens Committee for the Right to Keep and Bear Arms

Preventing Crime in Urban Communities: Handbook and Program Profiles—National Crime Prevention Council

Quarterly Economic Report on the African American Worker (quarterly)—National Urban League, Inc.

Report on Organized Crime (1970)—Pennsylvania Crime Commission

Report on Organized Crime (1980)—Pennsylvania Crime Commission

Report on Organized Crime: A Decade of Change (1990)—Pennsylvania Crime Commission

Research Findings (annually)—National Association of Criminal Justice Planners

The Rights of Gun Owners—Citizens Committee for the Right to Keep and Bear Arms

Right to Know—National Committee Against Repressive Legislation

Runta: The National Urban League Research Department Fact Sheet—National Urban League Inc.

A Step Toward Independence: Toward Economic Self-Sufficiency —National Coalition Against Domestic Violence

A Summary Review of Issues and Pending Legislation at the Federal Level in Subject

Areas Covered by the NGA/NCJA Survey on States' Organized Crime and Drug Trafficking Laws and Related Enforcement Tools—National Criminal Justice Association

Victim Assistance Programs and Resources (annually)—National Organization for Victim Assistance

Violence, Youth, and a Way Out—National Crime Prevention Council

Volunteer Newsletter (monthly)—SHANTI Project

The VORP Handbook—PACT Institute of Justice

WAR Newsletter (quarterly)—Women Against Rape

Washington Digest (monthly)—National Association of Criminal Defense Lawyers

WE TIP Crimebusters (monthly)—WE TIP, Inc.

WE TIP Crimeline (quarterly)—WE TIP, Inc.

WE TIP's National Crimefighter—WE TIP, Inc.

Youth Law News (bimonthly)—National Center for Youth Law

CORRECTIONS

Accountability in Action (monthly)—American Restitution Association

ACRIM Newsletter—Association for Correctional Research and Information Managers

American Jails (bimonthly)—American Jail Association

"Americans Behind Bars: A Comparison of International Rates of Incarceration"—The Sentencing Project

Augustus: A Journal of Progressive Human Services (monthly)—National Center on Institutions and Alternatives

The California Prisoner—Prisoners' Rights Union

California Prisoner's Resource Guide—Prisoners' Rights Union

California State Prisoner's Handbook—Prisoners' Rights Union

CEA News and Notes (quarterly)—Correctional Education Association

The Correctional Psychologist—American Association for Correctional Psychology

Corrections Today (bimonthly)—American Correctional Association

Criminal Justice and Behavior (quarterly)—American Association for Correctional Psychology

CURE Newsletter (quarterly)—Citizens United for the Rehabilitation of Errants

Darkness Closes In: National Study of Jail Suicides—National Center on Institutions and Alternatives

Directory of Institutions—American Correctional Association

Directory of Residential Treatment Centers (biennially)—International Association of Residential and Community Alternatives

Directory of Restitution Programs (periodic)—American Restitution Association

Friends Outside (monthly)—Friends Outside

The Grapevine (bimonthly)—North American Association of Wardens and Superintendents

Guide to Juvenile Restitution—American Restitution Association

IARCA Journal (bimonthly)—International Association of Residential and Community Alternatives

Jail Operations Bulletin (monthly)—American Jail Association

Jails and Juvenile Facilities—Correctional Education Association

Journal for Juvenile Justice and Detention Services—National Association of Juvenile Correctional Agencies

Journal of Correctional Education (quarterly)—Correctional Education Association

Journal of Prisoners on Prisons (quarterly)—Journal of Prisoners on Prisons

Juvenile Decarceration: The Politics of Correctional Reform—National Center on Institutions and Alternatives

Learning Behind Bars: Selected Educational Programs in Prisons—Correctional Education Association

NAJCA News (quarterly)—National Association of Juvenile Correctional Agencies

National Jail and Adult Detention Directory—American Correctional Association

National Prison Project Journal (quarterly)—National Prison Project of the ACLU

On the Line—American Correctional Association

Prisoner's Assistance Directory (annually)—National Prison Project of the ACLU

Proceedings (annually)—National Association of Juvenile Correctional Agencies

Scared Straight: A Second Look—National Center on Institutions and Alternatives

Status Report on the Courts and the Prisons (annually)—National Prison Project of the ACLU

Staying Together (three times yearly)—Aid to Incarcerated Mothers

"Young Black Men and the Criminal Justice System: A Growing National Problem"— The Sentencing Project

JUDICIAL

AJA Benchmark (quarterly)—American Judges Association

Annual Report (annually)—National Center for State Courts

Court Review (quarterly)—American Judges Association

Journal and Family Court Newsletter (bimonthly)—National Council of Juvenile and Family Court Judges

Judicature (quarterly)—American Judicature Society

Judicial Conduct Reporter (quarterly)—American Judicature Society

Judicial Salary Review (semiannually)—National Center for State Courts

Juvenile and Family Court Journal (quarterly)—National Council of Juvenile and Family Court Judges

Juvenile and Family Law Digest (monthly)—National Council of Juvenile and Family Court Judges

National Council on Juvenile and Family Court Judges–Directory (annually)—National Council of Juvenile and Family Court Judges

Report (monthly)—National Center for State Courts

State Court Journal (monthly)—National Center for State Courts

LAW ENFORCEMENT

The Caller (monthly)—Crime Stoppers International

Directory (annually)—Crime Stoppers International

Directory of IACP Members (annually)—International Association of Chiefs of Police

Federal Criminal Investigator (quarterly)—Federal Criminal Investigators Association

Jail and Prisoner Law Bulletin (monthly)—Americans for Effective Law Enforcement

The Journal (quarterly)—Fraternal Order of Police

Law Enforcement Legal Liability Reporter (monthly)—Americans for Effective Law Enforcement

Police Chief: The Professional View of Law Enforcement (monthly)—International Association of Chiefs of Police

The Pro-Gram (monthly)—Federal Criminal Investigators Association

Security Legal Update (monthly)—Americans for Effective Law Enforcement

LEGISLATIVE/GOVERNMENTAL

Annual Report (annually)—The U.S. Conference of Mayors

Federal Funds Information for States—National Governor's Association

Federal Update (bimonthly)—National Conference of State Legislators

Fiscal Letter (bimonthly)—National Conference of State Legislators

Governor's Weekly Bulletin (weekly)—National Governor's Association

Policy Positions (semiannually)—National Governor's Association

President's Budget: Impact on the States (annually)—National Governor's Association

State Legislatures (ten times per year)—National Conference of State Legislators

RELIGIOUS

Annual Report (annually)—American Friends Service Committee

Anti-Defamation League Bulletin (quarterly)—Anti-Defamation League of B'nai B'rith

Beyond Crime and Punishment: Restorative Justice—Justice Fellowship

Briefly (monthly)—Christian Legal Society

Conciliation Quarterly (quarterly)—Mennonite Central Committee

Convicted: New Hope for Ending America's Crime Crisis—Justice Fellowship

Crime and Community and Biblical Perspective—Judicial Process Commission

Dimensions (quarterly)—Anti-Defamation League of B'nai B'rith

Draft Counselor's Update—Mennonite Central Committee

Face-to-Face Interreligious Bulletin (quarterly)—Anti-Defamation League of B'nai B'rith

The Genesee Conciliator (bimonthly)—Judicial Process Commission

Hope, Respect, Reconciliation: A Christian Response to Gun Violence—Presbyterian Criminal Justice Program

Intercessor (quarterly)—Christian Legal Society

Is There a Better Way?: A Case for Alternatives to Prison —Justice Fellowship

Justice Jottings (annually)—Presbyterian Criminal Justice Program

The Justice Report (quarterly)—Justice Fellowship

Justicia (quarterly)—Judicial Process Commission

Juvenile Justice: Involvement for Christians—Presbyterian Criminal Justice Program

Lawyer's Forum (quarterly)—Christian Legal Society

Life Sentence—Justice Fellowship

Lineage and Other Stories—Prison-Ashram Project

Mennonite Central Committee—Network Newsletter—Mennonite Central Committee

Middle East Insight (quarterly)—Anti-Defamation League of B'nai B'rith

Pastoral Ministry—U.S. Catholic Conference

"Position Paper on Deadly Force"—Judicial Process Commission

Prison Evangelism Magazine (quarterly)—International Prison Ministry

Prison Ministry Yoke News (quarterly)—Yokefellowship International Prison Ministries

Quaker Service Bulletin (semiannually)—American Friends Service Committee

Quarterly (quarterly)—Christian Legal Society

Restorative Justice: Toward Nonviolence—Judicial Process Commission

Transfiguration Prison Ministry (quarterly)—(Society of the) Transfiguration Prison Ministries

Transfiguration Quarterly (quarterly)—(Society of the) Transfiguration Prison Ministries

UPDATE—John Howard Association

USCC Currents (monthly)—U.S. Catholic Conference

We're All Doing Time—Prison-Ashram Project

Yokefellowship Prison Ministry Directory (annually)—Yokefellowship International Prison Ministries

Young People and the Death Penalty—Presbyterian Criminal Justice Program

SELECTED BIBLIOGRAPHY

———————————— / ————————————

Baker, Ralph, and Fred A. Meyer, Jr. 1980. *The Criminal Justice Game: Politics and Players*. North Scituate, MA: Duxbury Press.

Berk, Richard A., and Peter H. Rossi. 1977. *Prison Reform and State Elites*. Cambridge, MA: Ballinger Publishing Co.

Brownmiller, Susan. 1975. *Against Our Will: Men, Women and Rape*. New York: Simon and Schuster.

Fairchild, Ereka S. 1981. "Interest Groups in the Criminal Justice Process." *Journal of Criminal Justice* 9: 181–194.

Esltp, Rhoda, and Patrick T. Macdonald. 1984. "How Prime-Time Crime Evolved on TV, 1976 to 1983." In *Justice and the Media: Issues and Research*, ed. Ray Sukette. Springfield, IL: Charles C. Thomas.

Feeley, Malcolm M., and Austin D. Sarat. 1980. *The Policy Dilemma: Federal Crime Policy and the Law Enforcement Assistance Administration, 1968–1978*. Minneapolis: University of Minnesota Press.

Graber, Doris. 1980. *Crime News and the Public*. New York: Praeger.

Gray, Virginia, and Bruce Williams. 1980. *The Organizational Politics of Criminal Justice*. Lexington, MA: Lexington Books.

Gusfield, Joseph R. 1963. *Symbolic Crusade: Status Politics and the American Temperance Movement*. Chicago: University of Illinois.

Jacob, Herbert. 1984. *The Frustration of Policy: Responses to Crime in American Cities*. Boston: Little, Brown.

La Free, Gary D. 1989. *Rape and Criminal Justice: The Social Construction of Sexual Assault*. Belmont, CA: Wadsworth.

Leddy, Edward F. 1987. *Magnum Force Lobby: The National Rifle Association Fights Gun Control*. New York: Lanham.

Nagel, Stuart, Erika Fairchild, and Anthony Champagne, eds. 1983. *The Political Science of Criminal Justice*. Springfield, IL: Charles C. Thomas.

Olson, Susan M. 1990. "Interest Group Litigation in Federal District Court: Beyond the Political Disadvantage Theory." *Journal of Politics* 52, 3: 854–882.

Pleck, Elizabeth. 1987. *Domestic Tyranny*. New York: Oxford University Press.
Stolz, Barbara Ann. (1984, January). ''Interest Groups and Criminal Law: The Case of Federal Criminal Code Revision.'' *Crime and Delinquency* 30, 1: 91–106.

INDEX

————————— / —————————

ABOUT THE AUTHORS

MICHAEL A. HALLETT is Assistant Professor of Criminal Justice Administration at Middle Tennessee State University. He has published a number of
articles in journals on subjects ranging from news media coverage of the HIV/
AIDS crisis to the "politics" of criminal justice program evaluation.

DENNIS J. PALUMBO is Professor in the School of Justice Studies and Director
of the Ph.D. Program in Justice Studies at Arizona State University. He has
written at length on criminal justice, public policy, and public administration.
His books include *Contemporary Public Administration* (1991), *Implementation
and the Policy Process: Opening up the Black Box* (Greenwood Press, 1990),
and *Criminal Justice in America: Law in Action* (1986).